Hammond World Atlas

WORLD REFERENCE GUIDE

 These four pages contain flags and important facts about each independent country in the world, including page reference, area, population and capital.

MAPS

 New maps, derived from a computer database, accurately present political detail while proprietary map projections show the most distortion-free views of the continents. Numbers following each entry indicate map scale (M = million).

INDEX

 A 1,200-entry A to Z index lists major places and geographic features in the atlas, complete with page numbers and easy-to-use alpha-numeric references.

SYMBOLS USED ON MAPS

 The list below defines the principal symbols used to denote line, area and point features in this atlas.

- ═══ National Boundary
- ▬▬ Internal Boundary
- ········· Undefined Boundary
- Rome National Capital
- Belfast Other Capital
- ─── Shoreline, River
- ·─·─· Intermittent River
- ········ Canal
- ⬭ Lake, Reservoir
- ⬭ Intermittent Lake
- ▲ Point Elevation
- ⫯ Pass
- ⸫ Ruins
- • Dam
- ● Falls
- ■ Point of Interest

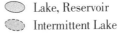

World Flags and Reference Guide

Afghanistan 21/H2
Area: 250,000 sq. mi.
  647,500 sq. km.
Population: 21,251,821
Capital: Kabul

Albania 13/H3
Area: 11,100 sq. mi.
  28,749 sq. km.
Population: 3,413,904
Capital: Tiranë

Algeria 44/F2
Area: 919,591 sq. mi.
  2,381,740 sq. km.
Population: 28,539,321
Capital: Algiers

Andorra 12/D3
Area: 174 sq. mi.
  450 sq. km.
Population: 65,780
Capital: Andorra la Vella

Angola 46/C3
Area: 481,351 sq. mi.
  1,246,700 sq. km.
Population: 10,069,501
Capital: Luanda

Antigua & Barbuda 36/F3
Area: 170 sq. mi.
  440 sq. km.
Population: 65,176
Capital: St. John's

Argentina 42/C4
Area: 1,068,296 sq. mi.
  2,766,890 sq. km.
Population: 34,292,742
Capital: Buenos Aires

Armenia 15/F5
Area: 11,506 sq. mi.
  29,800 sq. km.
Population: 3,557,284
Capital: Yerevan

Australia 29
Area: 2,967,893 sq. mi.
  7,686,850 sq. km.
Population: 18,322,231
Capital: Canberra

Austria 13/G2
Area: 32,375 sq. mi.
  83,851 sq. km.
Population: 7,986,664
Capital: Vienna

Azerbaijan 15/G5
Area: 33,436 sq. mi.
  86,600 sq. km.
Population: 7,789,886
Capital: Baku

Bahamas 36/E2
Area: 5,382 sq. mi.
  13,939 sq. km.
Population: 256,616
Capital: Nassau

Bahrain 20/F3
Area: 240 sq. mi.
  622 sq. km.
Population: 575,925
Capital: Manama

Bangladesh 22/E3
Area: 55,598 sq. mi.
  144,000 sq. km.
Population: 128,094,948
Capital: Dhaka

Barbados 36/F3
Area: 166 sq. mi.
  430 sq. km.
Population: 256,395
Capital: Bridgetown

Belarus 11/L3
Area: 80,154 sq. mi.
  207,600 sq. km.
Population: 10,437,418
Capital: Minsk

Belgium 10/E4
Area: 11,780 sq. mi.
  30,510 sq. km.
Population: 10,081,880
Capital: Brussels

Belize 36/D3
Area: 8,865 sq. mi.
  22,960 sq. km.
Population: 214,061
Capital: Belmopan

Benin 44/F5
Area: 43,483 sq. mi.
  112,620 sq. km.
Population: 5,522,677
Capital: Porto-Novo

Bhutan 22/E2
Area: 18,147 sq. mi.
  47,000 sq. km.
Population: 1,780,638
Capital: Thimphu

Bolivia 40/F7
Area: 424,163 sq. mi.
  1,098,582 sq. km.
Population: 7,896,254
Capital: La Paz; Sucre

Bosnia & Herz. 13/H2
Area: 19,781 sq. mi.
  51,233 sq. km.
Population: 3,201,823
Capital: Sarajevo

Botswana 46/D5
Area: 231,803 sq. mi.
  600,370 sq. km.
Population: 1,392,414
Capital: Gaborone

Brazil 40/F5
Area: 3,286,470 sq. mi.
  8,511,965 sq. km.
Population: 160,737,489
Capital: Brasília

Brunei 26/D2
Area: 2,228 sq. mi.
  5,770 sq. km.
Population: 292,266
Cap: Bandar Seri Begawan

Bulgaria 13/K3
Area: 42,823 sq. mi.
  110,912 sq. km.
Population: 8,775,198
Capital: Sofia

Burkina 44/E5
Area: 105,869 sq. mi.
  274,200 sq. km.
Population: 10,422,828
Capital: Ouagadougou

Burundi 46/E1
Area: 10,745 sq. mi.
  27,830 sq. km.
Population: 6,262,429
Capital: Bujumbura

Cambodia 23/H5
Area: 69,900 sq. mi.
  181,040 sq. km.
Population: 10,561,373
Capital: Phnom Penh

Cameroon 44/H7
Area: 183,568 sq. mi.
  475,441 sq. km.
Population: 13,521,000
Capital: Yaoundé

Canada 37
Area: 3,851,787 sq. mi.
  9,976,139 sq. km.
Population: 28,434,545
Capital: Ottawa

Cape Verde 6/H5
Area: 1,556 sq. mi.
  4,030 sq. km.
Population: 435,983
Capital: Praia

Central African Rep. 45/J6
Area: 240,533 sq. mi.
  622,980 sq. km.
Population: 3,209,759
Capital: Bangui

Chad 45/J4
Area: 495,752 sq. mi.
  1,283,998 sq. km.
Population: 5,586,505
Capital: N'Djamena

Chile 42/B3
Area: 292,258 sq. mi.
  756,950 sq. km.
Population: 14,161,216
Capital: Santiago

China 24/G5
Area: 3,705,386 sq. mi.
  9,596,960 sq. km.
Population: 1,203,097,268
Capital: Beijing

Colombia 40/D3
Area: 439,733 sq. mi.
  1,138,910 sq. km.
Population: 36,200,251
Capital: Bogotá

Comoros 7/M6
Area: 838 sq. mi.
  2,170 sq. km.
Population: 549,338
Capital: Moroni

Congo 44/H8
Area: 132,046 sq. mi.
  342,000 sq. km.
Population: 2,504,996
Capital: Brazzaville

Costa Rica 36/D4
Area: 19,730 sq. mi.
  51,100 sq. km.
Population: 3,419,114
Capital: San José

Côte d'Ivoire 44/D6
Area: 124,502 sq. mi.
  322,460 sq. km.
Population: 14,791,257
Capital: Yamoussoukro

Croatia 13/G2
Area: 22,050 sq. mi.
  56,538 sq. km.
Population: 4,665,821
Capital: Zagreb

Cuba 36/E2
Area: 42,803 sq. mi.
  110,860 sq. km.
Population: 10,937,635
Capital: Havana

Cyprus 20/B1
Area: 3,571 sq. mi.
  9,250 sq. km.
Population: 736,636
Capital: Nicosia

Czech Republic 11/H4
Area: 30,387 sq. mi.
  78,703 sq. km.
Population: 10,432,774
Capital: Prague

Denmark 10/G3
Area: 16,629 sq. mi.
  43,069 sq. km.
Population: 5,199,437
Capital: Copenhagen

Djibouti 45/P5
Area: 8,494 sq. mi.
  22,000 sq. km.
Population: 421,320
Capital: Djibouti

Dominica 36/F3
Area: 290 sq. mi.
  751 sq. km.
Population: 82,608
Capital: Roseau

Dominican Rep. 36/F3
Area: 18,815 sq. mi.
48,730 sq. km.
Population: 7,511,263
Capital: Santo Domingo

Ecuador 40/C4
Area: 109,483 sq. mi.
283,561 sq. km.
Population: 10,890,950
Capital: Quito

Egypt 45/L2
Area: 386,659 sq. mi.
1,001,447 sq. km.
Population: 62,359,623
Capital: Cairo

El Salvador 36/C3
Area: 8,124 sq. mi.
21,040 sq. km.
Population: 5,870,481
Capital: San Salvador

Equatorial Guinea 44/G7
Area: 10,831 sq. mi.
28,052 sq. km.
Population: 420,293
Capital: Malabo

Eritrea 45/N5
Area: 46,842 sq. mi.
121,320 sq. km.
Population: 3,578,709
Capital: Asmara

Estonia 11/L2
Area: 17,413 sq. mi.
45,100 sq. km.
Population: 1,625,399
Capital: Tallinn

Ethiopia 45/N5
Area: 435,184 sq. mi.
1,127,127 sq. km.
Population: 55,979,018
Capital: Addis Ababa

Fiji 30/G6
Area: 7,055 sq. mi.
18,272 sq. km.
Population: 772,891
Capital: Suva

Finland 14/H2
Area: 130,128 sq. mi.
337,032 sq. km.
Population: 5,085,206
Capital: Helsinki

France 12/D2
Area: 211,208 sq. mi.
547,030 sq. km.
Population: 58,109,160
Capital: Paris

Gabon 44/H7
Area: 103,347 sq. mi.
267,670 sq. km.
Population: 1,155,749
Capital: Libreville

Gambia 44/B5
Area: 4,363 sq. mi.
11,300 sq. km.
Population: 989,273
Capital: Banjul

Georgia 15/F5
Area: 26,911 sq. mi.
69,700 sq. km.
Population: 5,725,972
Capital: T'bilisi

Germany 10/G4
Area: 137,803 sq. mi.
356,910 sq. km.
Population: 81,337,541
Capital: Berlin

Ghana 44/E6
Area: 92,100 sq. mi.
238,540 sq. km.
Population: 17,763,138
Capital: Accra

Greece 13/J4
Area: 50,942 sq. mi.
131,940 sq. km.
Population: 10,647,511
Capital: Athens

Grenada 36/F3
Area: 131 sq. mi.
340 sq. km.
Population: 94,486
Capital: St. George's

Guatemala 36/C3
Area: 42,042 sq. mi.
108,889 sq. km.
Population: 10,998,602
Capital: Guatemala

Guinea 44/C5
Area: 94,927 sq. mi.
245,860 sq. km.
Population: 6,549,336
Capital: Conakry

Guinea-Bissau 44/B5
Area: 13,946 sq. mi.
36,120 sq. km.
Population: 1,124,537
Capital: Bissau

Guyana 40/G3
Area: 83,000 sq. mi.
214,970 sq. km.
Population: 723,774
Capital: Georgetown

Haiti 36/E3
Area: 10,714 sq. mi.
27,750 sq. km.
Population: 6,539,983
Capital: Port-au-Prince

Honduras 36/D3
Area: 43,277 sq. mi.
112,087 sq. km.
Population: 5,459,743
Capital: Tegucigalpa

Hungary 13/H2
Area: 35,919 sq. mi.
93,030 sq. km.
Population: 10,318,838
Capital: Budapest

Iceland 14/N7
Area: 39,768 sq. mi.
103,000 sq. km.
Population: 265,998
Capital: Reykjavík

India 19/G7
Area: 1,269,339 sq. mi.
3,287,588 sq. km.
Population: 936,545,814
Capital: New Delhi

Indonesia 27/E4
Area: 741,096 sq. mi.
1,919,440 sq. km.
Population: 203,583,886
Capital: Jakarta

Iran 19/E6
Area: 636,293 sq. mi.
1,648,000 sq. km.
Population: 64,625,455
Capital: Tehran

Iraq 20/D2
Area: 168,753 sq. mi.
437,072 sq. km.
Population: 20,643,769
Capital: Baghdad

Ireland 10/B3
Area: 27,136 sq. mi.
70,282 sq. km.
Population: 3,550,448
Capital: Dublin

Israel 20/B2
Area: 8,019 sq. mi.
20,770 sq. km.
Population: 5,433,134
Capital: Jerusalem

Italy 13/F3
Area: 116,305 sq. mi.
301,230 sq. km.
Population: 58,261,971
Capital: Rome

Jamaica 36/E3
Area: 4,243 sq. mi.
10,990 sq. km.
Population: 2,574,291
Capital: Kingston

Japan 25/P4
Area: 145,882 sq. mi.
377,835 sq. km.
Population: 125,506,492
Capital: Tokyo

Jordan 20/C2
Area: 34,445 sq. mi.
89,213 sq. km.
Population: 4,100,709
Capital: Amman

Kazakstan 16/G5
Area: 1,049,150 sq. mi.
2,717,300 sq. km.
Population: 17,376,615
Capital: Aqmola

Kenya 45/N7
Area: 224,960 sq. mi.
582,646 sq. km.
Population: 28,817,227
Capital: Nairobi

Kiribati 30/H5
Area: 277 sq. mi.
717 sq. km.
Population: 79,386
Capital: Tarawa

Korea, North 25/N3
Area: 46,540 sq. mi.
120,539 sq. km.
Population: 23,486,550
Capital: P'yŏngyang

Korea, South 25/N4
Area: 38,023 sq. mi.
98,480 sq. km.
Population: 45,553,882
Capital: Seoul

Kuwait 20/E3
Area: 6,880 sq. mi.
17,820 sq. km.
Population: 1,817,397
Capital: Kuwait

Kyrgyzstan 16/H5
Area: 76,641 sq. mi.
198,500 sq. km.
Population: 4,769,877
Capital: Bishkek

Laos 23/H3
Area: 91,428 sq. mi.
236,800 sq. km.
Population: 4,837,237
Capital: Vientiane

Latvia 11/L2
Area: 24,749 sq. mi.
64,100 sq. km.
Population: 2,762,899
Capital: Riga

Lebanon 20/C2
Area: 4,015 sq. mi.
10,399 sq. km.
Population: 3,695,921
Capital: Beirut

Lesotho 46/E6
Area: 11,718 sq. mi.
30,350 sq. km.
Population: 1,992,960
Capital: Maseru

Liberia 44/D6
Area: 43,000 sq. mi.
111,370 sq. km.
Population: 3,073,245
Capital: Monrovia

Note – Page and letter-number references in blue type follow the country names. For example: **Bulgaria** 13/K3 refers to page 13, index grid square K3.

World Flags and Reference Guide

Libya 45/J2
Area: 679,358 sq. mi.
1,759,537 sq. km.
Population: 5,248,401
Capital: Tripoli

Liechtenstein 13/F2
Area: 62 sq. mi.
160 sq. km.
Population: 30,654
Capital: Vaduz

Lithuania 11/K3
Area: 25,174 sq. mi.
65,200 sq. km.
Population: 3,876,396
Capital: Vilnius

Luxembourg 10/F4
Area: 999 sq. mi.
2,587 sq. km.
Population: 404,660
Capital: Luxembourg

Macedonia 13/J3
Area: 9,781 sq. mi.
25,333 sq. km.
Population: 2,159,503
Capital: Skopje

Madagascar 46/K10
Area: 226,657 sq. mi.
587,041 sq. km.
Population: 13,862,325
Capital: Antananarivo

Malawi 46/F3
Area: 45,745 sq. mi.
118,480 sq. km.
Population: 9,808,384
Capital: Lilongwe

Malaysia 26/C2
Area: 127,316 sq. mi.
329,750 sq. km.
Population: 19,723,587
Capital: Kuala Lumpur

Maldives 19/G9
Area: 116 sq. mi.
300 sq. km.
Population: 261,310
Capital: Male

Mali 44/E4
Area: 478,764 sq. mi.
1,240,000 sq. km.
Population: 9,375,132
Capital: Bamako

Malta 13/G5
Area: 124 sq. mi.
320 sq. km.
Population: 369,609
Capital: Valletta

Marshall Islands 30/G3
Area: 70 sq. mi.
181 sq. km.
Population: 56,157
Capital: Majuro

Mauritania 44/C4
Area: 397,953 sq. mi.
1,030,700 sq. km.
Population: 2,263,202
Capital: Nouakchott

Mauritius 7/M7
Area: 718 sq. mi.
1,860 sq. km.
Population: 1,127,068
Capital: Port Louis

Mexico 36/B2
Area: 761,601 sq. mi.
1,972,546 sq. km.
Population: 93,985,848
Capital: Mexico City

Micronesia 30/D4
Area: 271 sq. mi.
702 sq. km.
Population: 122,950
Capital: Kolonia

Moldova 11/L5
Area: 13,012 sq. mi.
33,700 sq. km.
Population: 4,489,657
Capital: Chişinău

Monaco 12/E3
Area: 0.7 sq. mi.
1.9 sq. km.
Population: 31,515
Capital: Monaco

Mongolia 24/G2
Area: 606,163 sq. mi.
1,569,962 sq. km.
Population: 2,493,615
Capital: Ulaanbaatar

Morocco 44/C1
Area: 172,414 sq. mi.
446,550 sq. km.
Population: 29,168,848
Capital: Rabat

Mozambique 46/G4
Area: 309,494 sq. mi.
801,590 sq. km.
Population: 18,115,250
Capital: Maputo

Myanmar (Burma) 23/G3
Area: 261,969 sq. mi.
678,500 sq. km.
Population: 45,103,809
Capital: Yangon (Rangoon)

Namibia 46/C5
Area: 318,694 sq. mi.
825,418 sq. km.
Population: 1,651,545
Capital: Windhoek

Nauru 30/F5
Area: 8 sq. mi.
21 sq. km.
Population: 10,149
Capital: Yaren (district)

Nepal 22/D2
Area: 54,363 sq. mi.
140,800 sq. km.
Population: 21,560,869
Capital: Kathmandu

Netherlands 10/F3
Area: 14,413 sq. mi.
37,330 sq. km.
Population: 15,452,903
Cap: The Hague; Amsterdam

New Zealand 29/H6
Area: 103,736 sq. mi.
268,676 sq. km.
Population: 3,660,364
Capital: Wellington

Nicaragua 36/D3
Area: 49,998 sq. mi.
129,494 sq. km.
Population: 4,206,353
Capital: Managua

Niger 44/G4
Area: 489,189 sq. mi.
1,267,000 sq. km.
Population: 9,280,208
Capital: Niamey

Nigeria 44/G6
Area: 356,668 sq. mi.
923,770 sq. km.
Population: 101,232,251
Capital: Abuja

Norway 14/C3
Area: 125,181 sq. mi.
324,220 sq. km.
Population: 4,330,951
Capital: Oslo

Oman 21/G4
Area: 82,031 sq. mi.
212,460 sq. km.
Population: 2,125,089
Capital: Muscat

Pakistan 21/H3
Area: 310,403 sq. mi.
803,944 sq. km.
Population: 131,541,920
Capital: Islamabad

Palau 30/C4
Area: 177 sq. mi.
458 sq. km.
Population: 16,661
Capital: Koror

Panama 36/D4
Area: 30,193 sq. mi.
78,200 sq. km.
Population: 2,680,903
Capital: Panamá

Papua New Guinea 30/D5
Area: 178,259 sq. mi.
461,690 sq. km.
Population: 4,294,750
Capital: Port Moresby

Paraguay 42/E1
Area: 157,047 sq. mi.
406,752 sq. km.
Population: 5,358,198
Capital: Asunción

Peru 40/C5
Area: 496,223 sq. mi.
1,285,220 sq. km.
Population: 24,087,372
Capital: Lima

Philippines 31/S10
Area: 115,830 sq. mi.
300,000 sq. km.
Population: 73,265,584
Capital: Manila

Poland 11/J3
Area: 120,725 sq. mi.
312,678 sq. km.
Population: 38,792,442
Capital: Warsaw

Portugal 12/A4
Area: 35,552 sq. mi.
92,080 sq. km.
Population: 10,562,388
Capital: Lisbon

Qatar 20/F3
Area: 4,247 sq. mi.
11,000 sq. km.
Population: 533,916
Capital: Doha

Romania 13/J2
Area: 91,699 sq. mi.
237,500 sq. km.
Population: 23,198,330
Capital: Bucharest

Russia 16/H3
Area: 6,592,735 sq. mi.
17,075,200 sq. km.
Population: 149,909,089
Capital: Moscow

Rwanda 46/E1
Area: 10,169 sq. mi.
26,337 sq. km.
Population: 8,605,307
Capital: Kigali

Saint Kitts & Nevis 36/F3
Area: 104 sq. mi.
269 sq. km.
Population: 40,992
Capital: Basseterre

Saint Lucia 36/F3
Area: 239 sq. mi.
620 sq. km.
Population: 156,050
Capital: Castries

St. Vinc. & Grens. 36/F3
Area: 131 sq. mi.
340 sq. km.
Population: 117,344
Capital: Kingstown

5

 San Marino 13/G3
Area: 23.4 sq. mi.
60.6 sq. km.
Population: 24,313
Capital: San Marino

 São Tomé & Prín. 44/F7
Area: 371 sq. mi.
960 sq. km.
Population: 140,423
Capital: São Tomé

 Saudi Arabia 20/D4
Area: 756,981 sq. mi.
1,960,582 sq. km.
Population: 18,729,576
Capital: Riyadh

 Senegal 44/B5
Area: 75,749 sq. mi.
196,190 sq. km.
Population: 9,007,080
Capital: Dakar

 Seychelles 7/M6
Area: 176 sq. mi.
455 sq. km.
Population: 72,709
Capital: Victoria

Sierra Leone 44/C6
Area: 27,699 sq. mi.
71,740 sq. km.
Population: 4,753,120
Capital: Freetown

 Singapore 26/B3
Area: 244 sq. mi.
632.6 sq. km.
Population: 2,890,468
Capital: Singapore

 Slovakia 11/J4
Area: 18,859 sq. mi.
48,845 sq. km.
Population: 5,432,383
Capital: Bratislava

 Slovenia 13/G2
Area: 7,836 sq. mi.
20,296 sq. km.
Population: 2,051,522
Capital: Ljubljana

 Solomon Islands 30/E6
Area: 10,985 sq. mi.
28,450 sq. km.
Population: 399,206
Capital: Honiara

 Somalia 45/Q6
Area: 246,200 sq. mi.
637,658 sq. km.
Population: 7,347,554
Capital: Mogadishu

South Africa 46/D6
Area: 471,008 sq. mi.
1,219,912 sq. km.
Population: 45,095,459
Cap: Cape Town; Pretoria

 Spain 12/B3
Area: 194,884 sq. mi.
504,750 sq. km.
Population: 39,404,348
Capital: Madrid

 Sri Lanka 22/D6
Area: 25,332 sq. mi.
65,610 sq. km.
Population: 18,342,660
Capital: Colombo

 Sudan 45/L5
Area: 967,494 sq. mi.
2,505,809 sq. km.
Population: 30,120,420
Capital: Khartoum

 Suriname 41/G3
Area: 63,039 sq. mi.
163,270 sq. km.
Population: 429,544
Capital: Paramaribo

 Swaziland 46/F6
Area: 6,703 sq. mi.
17,360 sq. km.
Population: 966,977
Capital: Mbabane

 Sweden 14/E3
Area: 173,731 sq. mi.
449,964 sq. km.
Population: 8,821,759
Capital: Stockholm

 Switzerland 12/E2
Area: 15,943 sq. mi.
41,292 sq. km.
Population: 7,084,984
Capital: Bern

 Syria 20/C1
Area: 71,498 sq. mi.
185,180 sq. km.
Population: 15,451,917
Capital: Damascus

 Taiwan 25/M7
Area: 13,892 sq. mi.
35,980 sq. km.
Population: 21,500,583
Capital: Taipei

 Tajikistan 16/H6
Area: 55,251 sq. mi.
143,100 sq. km.
Population: 6,155,474
Capital: Dushanbe

 Tanzania 46/F2
Area: 364,699 sq. mi.
945,090 sq. km.
Population: 28,701,077
Capital: Dar es Salaam

Thailand 23/H4
Area: 198,455 sq. mi.
513,998 sq. km.
Population: 60,271,300
Capital: Bangkok

 Togo 44/F6
Area: 21,927 sq. mi.
56,790 sq. km.
Population: 4,410,370
Capital: Lomé

 Tonga 31/H7
Area: 289 sq. mi.
748 sq. km.
Population: 105,600
Capital: Nuku'alofa

 Trinidad & Tobago 40/F1
Area: 1,980 sq. mi.
5,128 sq. km.
Population: 1,271,159
Capital: Port-of-Spain

 Tunisia 44/G1
Area: 63,170 sq. mi.
163,610 sq. km.
Population: 8,879,845
Capital: Tunis

 Turkey 15/D6
Area: 301,382 sq. mi.
780,580 sq. km.
Population: 63,405,526
Capital: Ankara

 Turkmenistan 16/F6
Area: 188,455 sq. mi.
488,100 sq. km.
Population: 4,075,316
Capital: Ashgabat

 Tuvalu 30/G5
Area: 10 sq. mi.
26 sq. km.
Population: 9,991
Capital: Funafuti

 Uganda 45/M7
Area: 91,135 sq. mi.
236,040 sq. km.
Population: 19,573,262
Capital: Kampala

 Ukraine 15/C4
Area: 233,089 sq. mi.
603,700 sq. km.
Population: 51,867,828
Capital: Kiev

 United Arab Em. 20/F4
Area: 29,182 sq. mi.
75,581 sq. km.
Population: 2,924,594
Capital: Abu Dhabi

 United Kingdom 10/C3
Area: 94,525 sq. mi.
244,820 sq. km.
Population: 58,295,119
Capital: London

 United States 34
Area: 3,618,765 sq. mi.
9,372,610 sq. km.
Population: 266,661,112
Capital: Washington

 Uruguay 42/E3
Area: 68,039 sq. mi.
176,220 sq. km.
Population: 3,222,716
Capital: Montevideo

 Uzbekistan 16/G5
Area: 172,741 sq. mi.
447,400 sq. km.
Population: 23,089,261
Capital: Tashkent

 Vanuatu 30/F6
Area: 5,699 sq. mi.
14,760 sq. km.
Population: 173,648
Capital: Vila

 Vatican City 13/F3
Area: 0.17 sq. mi.
0.44 sq. km.
Population: 830
Capital: —

 Venezuela 40/E2
Area: 352,143 sq. mi.
912,050 sq. km.
Population: 21,004,773
Capital: Caracas

Vietnam 23/J5
Area: 127,243 sq. mi.
329,560 sq. km.
Population: 74,393,324
Capital: Hanoi

 Western Samoa 31/H6
Area: 1,104 sq. mi.
2,860 sq. km.
Population: 209,360
Capital: Apia

 Yemen 20/E5
Area: 203,849 sq. mi.
527,970 sq. km.
Population: 14,728,474
Capital: Sanaa

 Yugoslavia 13/J3
Area: 39,517 sq. mi.
102,350 sq. km.
Population: 11,101,833
Capital: Belgrade

 Zaire 46/D1
Area: 905,563 sq. mi.
2,345,410 sq. km.
Population: 44,060,636
Capital: Kinshasa

Zambia 46/E3
Area: 290,583 sq. mi.
752,610 sq. km.
Population: 9,445,723
Capital: Lusaka

 Zimbabwe 46/E4
Area: 150,803 sq. mi.
390,580 sq. km.
Population: 11,139,961
Capital: Harare

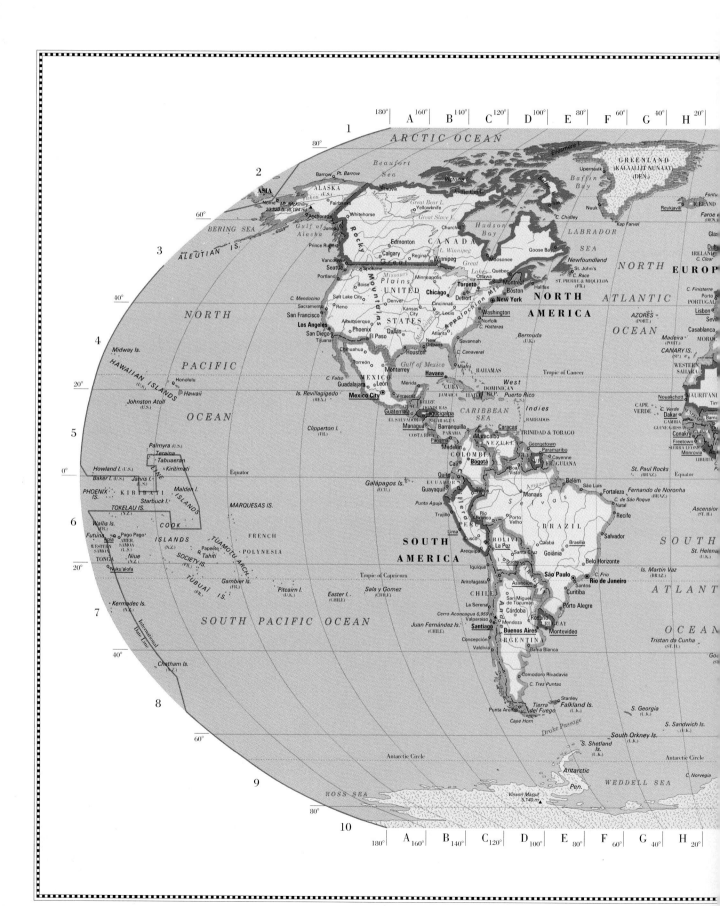

World

L 20° 40° M 60° N 80° P 100° Q 120° R 140° S 160° T 180°

FRANZ JOSEF LAND (RUS.)   ARCTIC OCEAN   Severnaya Zemlya   1

BARENTS SEA   Novaya Zemlya   Kara Sea   New Siberian Is.   2   80°

Hammerfest   North Cape   Murmansk   Khatanga   Noril'sk   Verkhoyansk   Arctic Circle

FINLAND   Archangel   Salekhard   Yenisey   Tura   Lena   Yakutsk   Magadan   Anadyr   60°

Stockholm   Syktyvkar   Surgut   Siberia   Lensk   BERING SEA   3

St. Petersburg   Nizhniy   Perm'   Yekaterinburg   Tomsk   Krasnoyarsk   Irkutsk   Chita   Okhotsk   Kamchatka   Petropavlovsk-Kamchatskiy   Int'l Date Line

Moscow   Novgorod   Chelyabinsk   Novosibirsk   Omsk   Ulan-Ude   Blagoveshchensk   Khabarovsk   Sakhalin   Mys Lopatka   KURIL IS.

Minsk   Voronezh   Kazan'   Ufa   RUSSIA   L. Baykal   Ulaanbaatar   Qiqihar   Harbin   Vladivostok   Sapporo   Hokkaido   40°   NORTH

Berlin   Warsaw   Kiev   Saratov   Samara   Magnitogorsk   Agmola   KAZAKSTAN   MONGOLIA   Gobi   Changchun   Shenyang   N. KOREA   Pyongyang   Sea of Japan   JAPAN   Honshu   PACIFIC

Prague   Kharkiv   Volgograd   Astrakhan'   Ozero Balkhash   Semey   Ürümqi   Baotou   Beijing   Tianjin   Dalian   Seoul   S. KOR.   Pusan   Kyōto   Tōkyō   Yokohama   4

Budapest   Rostov   El'brus 5,642 m   Almaty   Bishkek   Yumen   Takla Makan   Lanzhou   Taiyuan   CHINA   Xi'an   Huang   Jinan   Kyūshū   BONIN IS. (JAP.)

Belgrade   Bucharest   Black Sea   Istanbul   Ankara   Baku   Tashkent   Dushanbe   Tibet   Chengdu   Chongqing   Wuhan   Nanjing   Shanghai   EAST CHINA SEA   Taipei   VOLCANO IS. (JAP.)   Iwo Jima   Tropic of Cancer

Rome   Sofia   Athens   İzmir   TURKEY   Adana   ARMENIA   Tehrān   Mashhad   AFGHAN.   Kābul   Mt. Everest   Chasa   Changsha   Guiyang   Fuzhou   TAIWAN   RYUKYU IS.   20°

GREECE   CYPRUS   Damascus   IRAQ   IRAN   Eşfahān   Islāmābād   Lahore   Himalaya   Delhi   New Delhi   Kānpur   Ganges   Dhaka   Kunming   Guangzhou   HONG KONG (CHINA)   PHILIPPINE

Tripoli   Benghāzi   ISRAEL   Amman   Baghdad   Shīrāz   PAKISTAN   Hyderābād   Ahmadābād   Calcutta   MYANMAR   Mandalay   Hanoi   Hainan   C. Engaño   NORTHERN   SEA

LIBYA   Alexandria   Cairo   KUWAIT   Riyadh   BAHRAIN   QATAR   Karāchi   Muscat   INDIA   Bombay   Poona   BAY OF BENGAL   Yangon (Rangoon)   THAI-LAND   Vientiane   VIETNAM   Luzon   Manila   MARIANAS   Wake I. (U.S.)   OCEAN

Sabhā   EGYPT   Medina   SAUDI   ARABIA   Hyderābād   Bangalore   Madras   Bangkok   SOUTH   Manila   PHILIPPINES   Guam (U.S.)   Enewetak   Bikini   MARSHALL IS.   5

NIGER   CHAD   Zinder   Khartoum   Asmara   Sanaa   YEMEN   Socotra (YEMEN)   ARABIAN   SEA   Coimbatore   ANDAMAN AND NICOBAR IS. (INDIA)   CHINA   SEA   Phnom   Ho Chi Minh City   BRUNEI   Davao   PALAU   Koror   Truk Is.   Kwajalein   Majuro   Kotonia

N'Djamena   SUDAN   DJIBOUTI   Aden   Caseyr   C. Comorin   SRI LANKA   Colombo   Dondra Head   Kuala Lumpur   Mindanao   Yap Is.   CAROLINE IS.   MICRONESIA   Tarawa   KIRIBATI

ABUJA   CENTRAL AFRICAN REP.   Malakāl   Juba   ETHIOPIA   Addis Ababa   MALDIVES   Male   MALAYSIA   SINGA-PORE   Borneo   Celebes   Halmahera   Equator   NAURU   Banaba   0°

Yaoundé   Congo   Kisangani   Kampala   KENYA   Nairobi   Kilimanjaro 5,895 m   SEYCHELLES   INDIAN   BRITISH INDIAN OCEAN TERR.   Sumatra   Palembang   Java Sea   Jakarta   Celebes   Jayapura   New Guinea   New Ireland   New Britain   Bougainville   SOLOMON IS.   TUVALU

ZAIRE   RWANDA   BURUNDI   TANZANIA   Dar es Salaam   Aldabra Is. (SEY.)   Agalega Is. (MRTS.)   Diego Garcia   OCEAN   Bandung   Java   Ujung Pandang   Sumba   Timor   Arafura Sea   Torres Str.   PAPUA NEW GUINEA   Port Moresby   Guadalcanal   Honiara   Funafuti

Luanda   Kinshasa   Kananga   Lubumbashi   Lilongwe   COMOROS   Mayotte (FR.)   Antsiranana   Surabaya   CORAL   Sta. Cruz Is.   VANUATU   Rotuma I. (FIJI)   6

ANGOLA   Benguela   Huambo   ZAMBIA   Lusaka   Harare   MADAGASCAR   Mozambique Channel   Toamasina   Christmas I. (AUSTL.)   Cocos Is. (AUSTL.)   Darwin   Cape York Pen.   Cairns   SEA   New Caledonia (FR.)   Vila   FIJI   Suva   20°

C. Fria   NAMIBIA   ZIMBABWE   Beira   Antananarivo   Réunion (FR.)   MAURITIUS   Port Louis   Rodrigues (MRTS.)   Tropic of Capricorn   North West C.   Port Hedland   Great Sandy Desert   Alice Springs   Townsville   Rockhampton   Noumea   Loyalty Is.

Windhoek   BOTSWANA   Gaborone   Pretoria   Maputo   SWAZILAND   Toliara   Tanjona Vohimena   AUSTRALIA   Brisbane   Norfolk I. (AUSTL.)   7

Walvis Bay   Johannesburg   LESOTHO   Durban   Geraldton   Great Victoria Desert   Kalgoorlie   Whyalla   Great Australian Bight   Adelaide   Darling   Great Dividing Rge.   Newcastle   Sydney   Lord Howe I. (AUSTL.)   North C.

Cape Town   Bloemfontein   SOUTH AFRICA   Port Elizabeth   Perth   Albany   C. Leeuwin   Murray   Canberra   Mt. Kosciusko 2,228 m   Melbourne   TASMAN   Auckland   NEW   40°

Cape of Good Hope   C. Agulhas   Amsterdam I. (FR.)   St. Paul I. (FR.)   South East C.   Tasmania   Hobart   SEA   Wellington   ZEALAND   Christchurch   South I.

Prince Edward Is. (S. AFR.)   Crozet Is. (FR.)   Kerguélen (FR.)   McDonald Is. (AUSTL.)   Macquarie I. (AUSTL.)   Auckland Is. (N.Z.)   Antipodes Is. (N.Z.)   Campbell I. (N.Z.)   Dunedin   Bounty Is. (N.Z.)   8

C. Batterbee   Antarctic Circle   60°   80°   9

ANTARCTICA   ROSS SEA   C. Adare   10

L 20° 40° M 60° N 80° P 100° Q 120° R 140° S 160° T 180°

POPULATION OF CITIES AND TOWNS

⊚ OVER 5,000,000   ◉ 500,000 – 1,999,999
⊛ 2,000,000 – 4,999,999   ○ UNDER 500,000

SCALE 1:93,200,000   ROBINSON PROJECTION   STANDARD PARALLELS 38°N AND 38°S

MILES   0   1000   2000   3000   4000
KILOMETERS 0   1000   2000   3000   4000

Europe - Comparisons

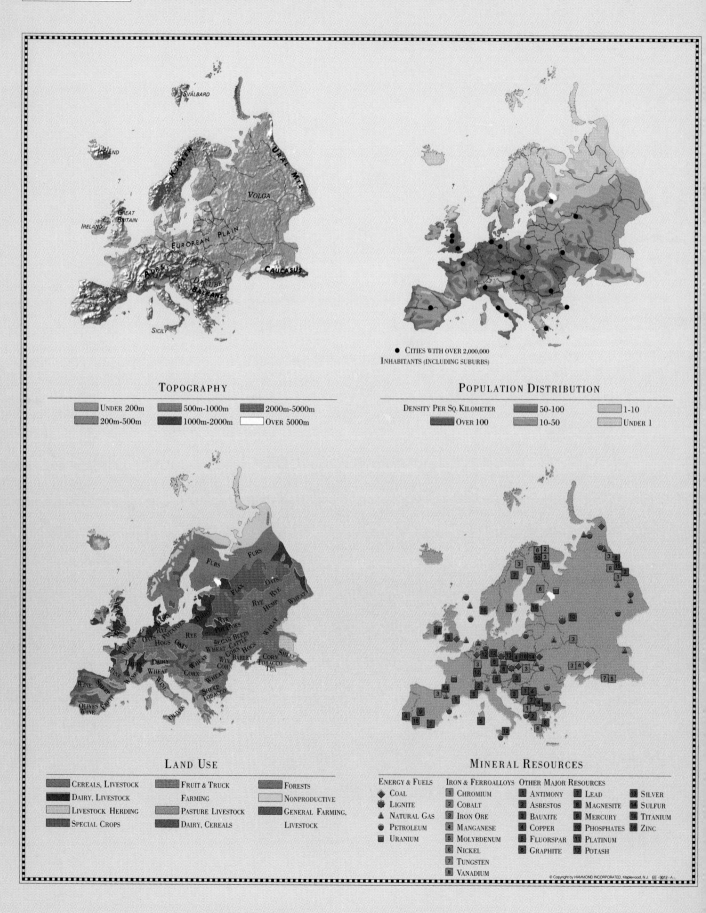

TOPOGRAPHY

Under 200m   500m-1000m   2000m-5000m

200m-500m   1000m-2000m   Over 5000m

POPULATION DISTRIBUTION

● CITIES WITH OVER 2,000,000
INHABITANTS (INCLUDING SUBURBS)

DENSITY PER SQ. KILOMETER   50-100   1-10

Over 100   10-50   Under 1

LAND USE

CEREALS, LIVESTOCK   FRUIT & TRUCK FARMING   FORESTS

DAIRY, LIVESTOCK   PASTURE LIVESTOCK   NONPRODUCTIVE

LIVESTOCK HERDING   DAIRY, CEREALS   GENERAL FARMING,

SPECIAL CROPS   LIVESTOCK

MINERAL RESOURCES

ENERGY & FUELS   IRON & FERROALLOYS   OTHER MAJOR RESOURCES

◆ COAL   1 CHROMIUM   1 ANTIMONY   7 LEAD   13 SILVER

◉ LIGNITE   2 COBALT   2 ASBESTOS   8 MAGNESITE   14 SULFUR

▲ NATURAL GAS   3 IRON ORE   3 BAUXITE   9 MERCURY   15 TITANIUM

● PETROLEUM   4 MANGANESE   4 COPPER   10 PHOSPHATES   16 ZINC

■ URANIUM   5 MOLYBDENUM   5 FLUORSPAR   11 PLATINUM

6 NICKEL   6 GRAPHITE   12 POTASH

7 TUNGSTEN

8 VANADIUM

Europe

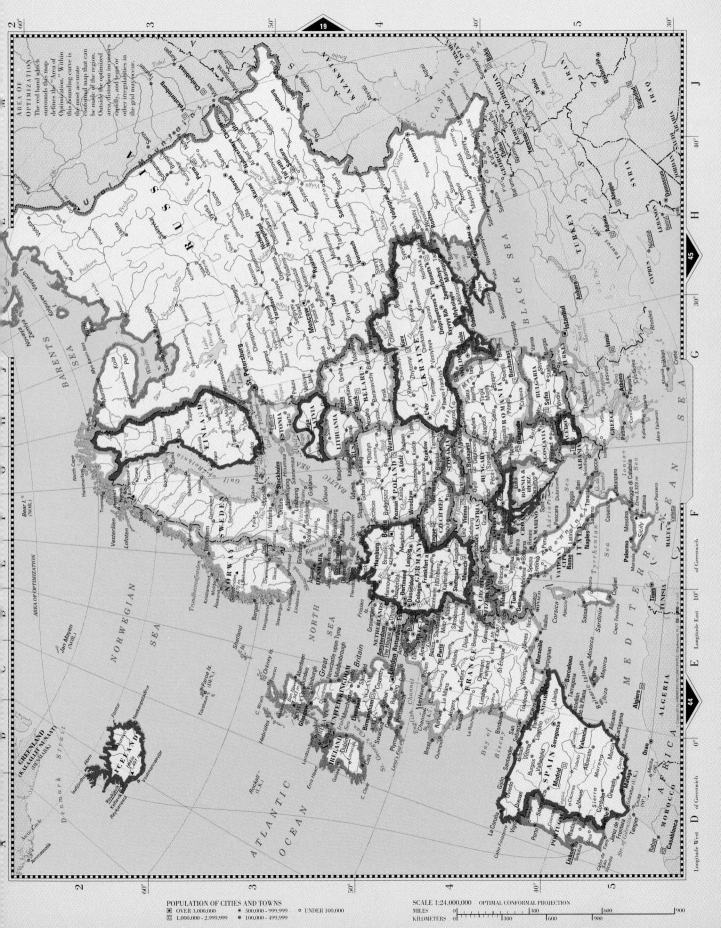

POPULATION OF CITIES AND TOWNS

▣ OVER 3,000,000 ⊙ 500,000–999,999 ○ UNDER 100,000
▢ 1,000,000–2,999,999 ⊙ 100,000–499,999

SCALE 1:24,000,000 OPTIMAL CONFORMAL PROJECTION

MILES 0 300 600 900
KILOMETERS 0 300 600 900

Western and Central Europe

Southern Europe

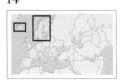

Scandinavia and
Finland, Iceland

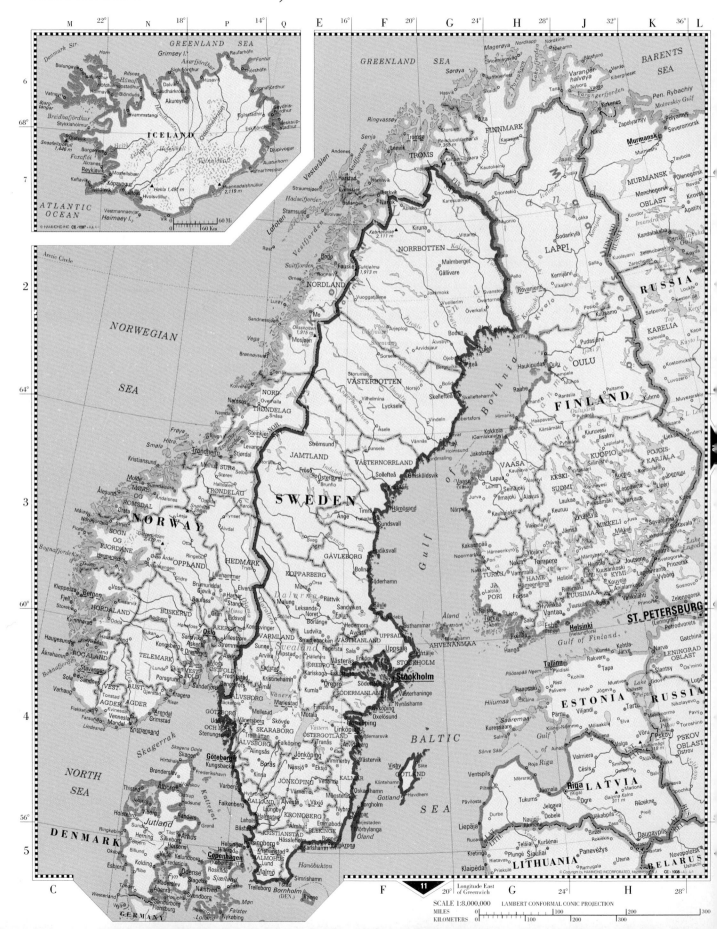

Eastern Europe and Turkey

POPULATION OF CITIES AND TOWNS

■ OVER 2,000,000   ▣ 500,000 - 999,999   ⊕ 100,000 - 249,999   ⊙ 10,000 - 29,999

▢ 1,000,000 - 1,999,999   ⊛ 250,000 - 499,999   ⊚ 30,000 - 99,999   ○ UNDER 10,000

SCALE 1:12,000,000   LAMBERT CONFORMAL CONIC PROJECTION

MILES   0   150   300

KILOMETERS   0   150   450

Longitude East of Greenwich

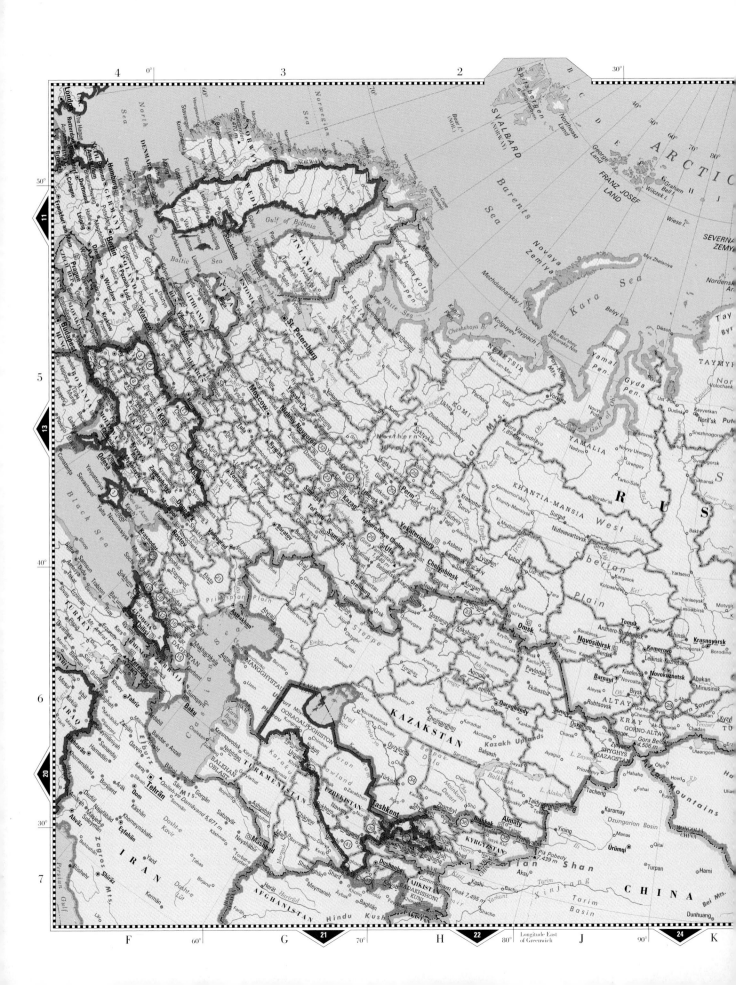

Russia and Neighboring Countries

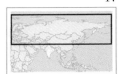

Administrative Divisions bear
same names as their respective
capitals, except:

Ukraine
1. Krym (Crimea)
2. Zakarpat
3. Volyn
4. Chernivets
5. Zaporiz
6. Rivnen
7. Ivano-Frankiv
8. Khmel'nyt
9. Cherka
10. Poltav
11. Chernivet

Georgia
12. Abkhazia
13. Ajaria

Azerbaijan
14. Nagorno-Karabakh

Russia
15. Dagestan
16. Ingushetia, Chechnya
17. North Ossetia
18. Kabardino-Balkaria
19. Karachay-Cherkessia
20. Adygea
21. Kalmykia
22. Mordovia
23. Chuvashia
24. Mari El
25. Tatarstan
26. Bashkortostan
27. Udmurtia
28. Permyakia
29. Khakassia
30. Ust'-Orda Buryat
31. Aga Buryat
32. Nizhnegorod

Kazakhstan
33. Soltustik Qazaqstan
34. Ongtustik Qazaqstan

Kyrgyzstan
35. Issyk-Kul' Oblast
36. Chuy

Tajikistan
37. Khatlon
38. Leninobad

Uzbekistan
39. Sirdaryo
40. Surkhondaryo
41. Qashqadaryo
42. Khorazm

POPULATION OF CITIES AND TOWNS
- ■ OVER 2,000,000
- ◉ 500,000 - 999,999
- ◎ 50,000 - 99,999
- ▣ 1,000,000 - 1,999,999
- ● 100,000 - 499,999
- ○ UNDER 50,000

SCALE 1:24,000,000   LAMBERT CONFORMAL CONIC PROJECTION

MILES   0   300   600   900

KILOMETERS   0   300   600   900

Asia - Comparisons

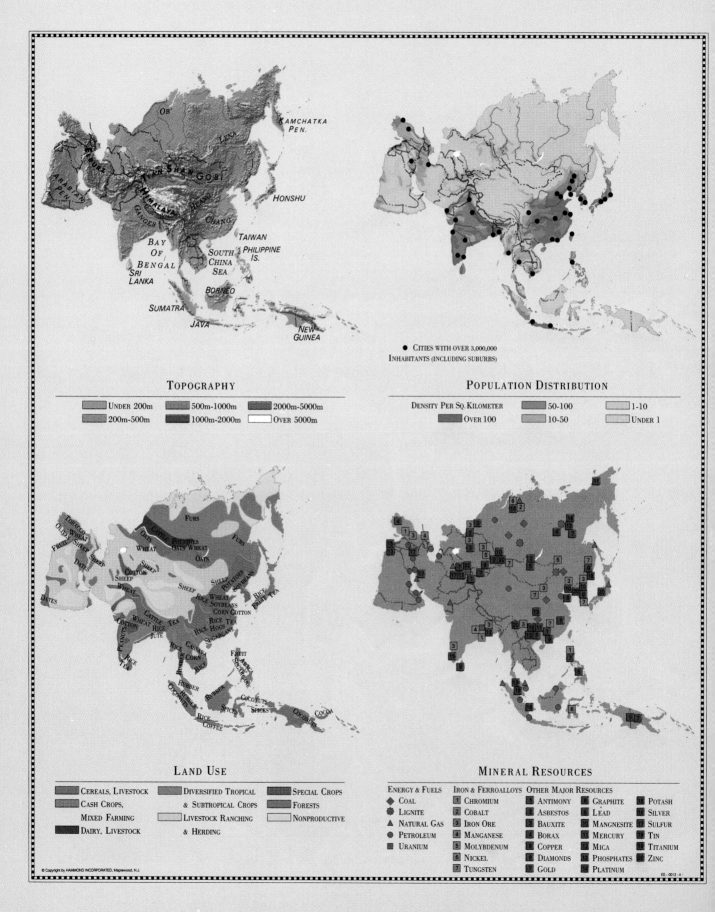

TOPOGRAPHY

▢ UNDER 200m	▢ 500m-1000m ▢ 2000m-5000m
▢ 200m-500m	▢ 1000m-2000m ▢ OVER 5000m

POPULATION DISTRIBUTION

● CITIES WITH OVER 3,000,000
INHABITANTS (INCLUDING SUBURBS)

DENSITY PER SQ. KILOMETER

OVER 100	▢ 50-100	▢ 1-10
	▢ 10-50	▢ UNDER 1

LAND USE

▢ CEREALS, LIVESTOCK	▢ DIVERSIFIED TROPICAL	▢ SPECIAL CROPS
▢ CASH CROPS,	& SUBTROPICAL CROPS	▢ FORESTS
MIXED FARMING	▢ LIVESTOCK RANCHING	▢ NONPRODUCTIVE
▢ DAIRY, LIVESTOCK	& HERDING	

© Copyright by HAMMOND INCORPORATED, Maplewood, N.J.

MINERAL RESOURCES

ENERGY & FUELS

- ◆ COAL
- ⬠ LIGNITE
- ▲ NATURAL GAS
- ● PETROLEUM
- ■ URANIUM

IRON & FERROALLOYS

1 CHROMIUM
2 COBALT
3 IRON ORE
4 MANGANESE
5 MOLYBDENUM
6 NICKEL
7 TUNGSTEN

OTHER MAJOR RESOURCES

1 ANTIMONY
2 ASBESTOS
3 BAUXITE
4 BORAX
5 COPPER
6 DIAMONDS
7 GOLD

8 GRAPHITE
9 LEAD
10 MANGNESITE
11 MERCURY
12 MICA
13 PHOSPHATES
14 PLATINUM

15 POTASH
16 SILVER
17 SULFUR
18 TIN
19 TITANIUM
20 ZINC

EE - 0013 - A

Asia

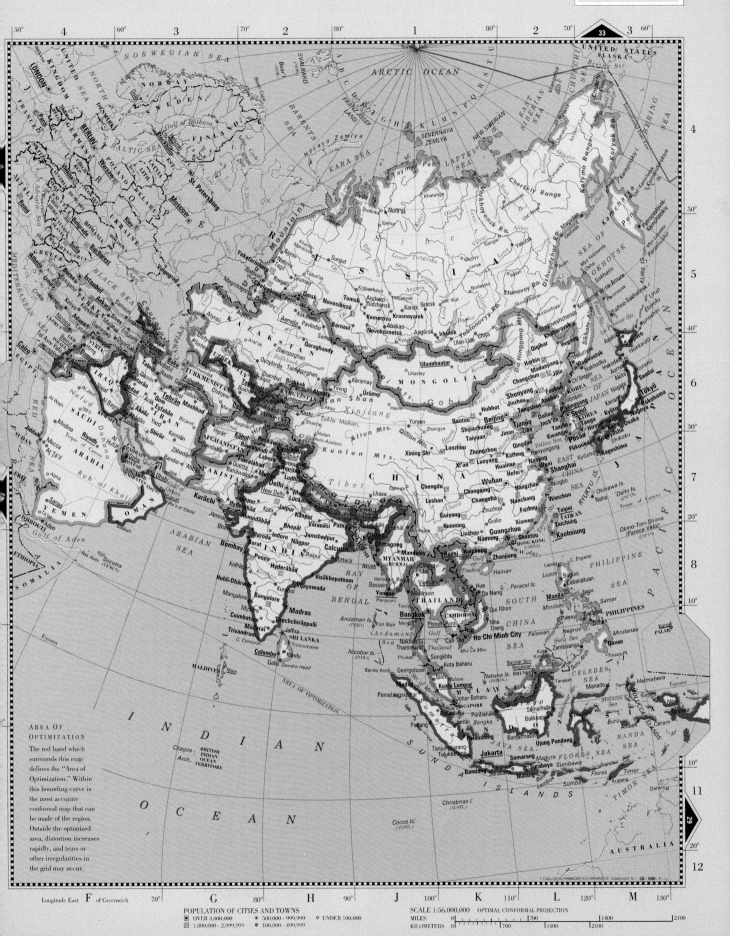

AREA OF
OPTIMIZATION

The red band which
surrounds this map
defines the "Area of
Optimization." Within
this bounding curve is
the most accurate
conformal map that can
be made of the region.
Outside the optimized
area, distortion increases
rapidly, and tears or
other irregularities in
the grid may occur.

POPULATION OF CITIES AND TOWNS

- ■ OVER 3,000,000
- ■ 1,000,000 - 2,999,999
- ● 500,000 - 999,999
- ● 100,000 - 499,999
- ○ UNDER 100,000

SCALE 1:56,000,000   OPTIMAL CONFORMAL PROJECTION

MILES 0 — 700 — 1400 — 2100
KILOMETERS 0 — 700 — 1400 — 2100

Longitude East F of Greenwich

© Copyright HAMMOND INCORPORATED, Maplewood, N.J.

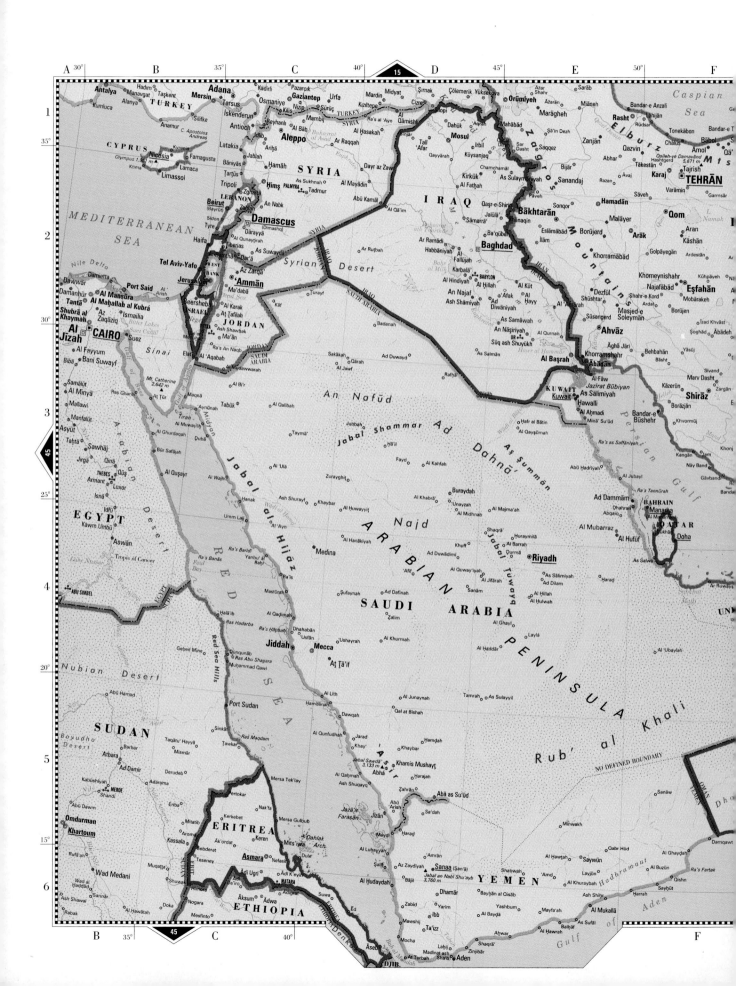

Southwestern Asia

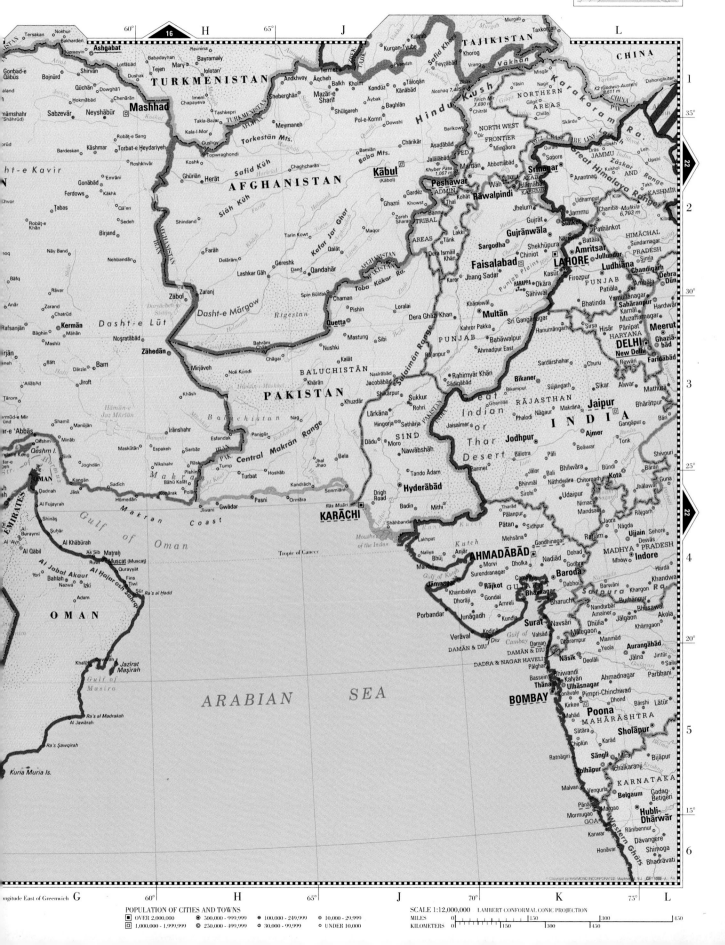

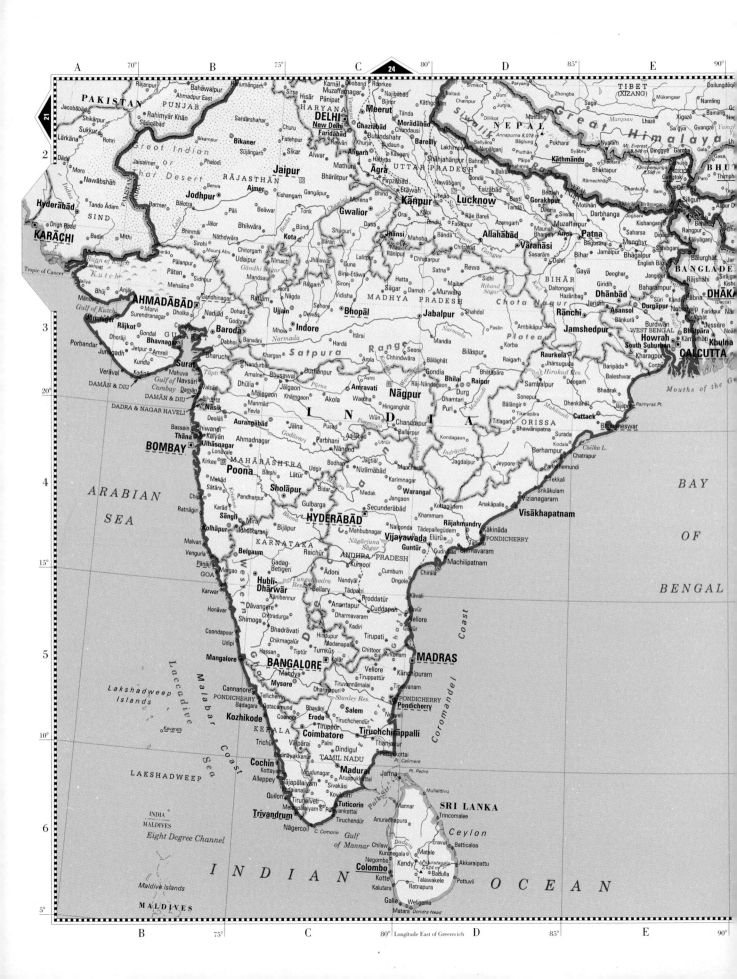

Southern Asia

POPULATION OF CITIES AND TOWNS

■ OVER 2,000,000	● 500,000 - 999,999	⊕ 100,000 - 249,999	○ 10,000 - 29,999
▢ 1,000,000 - 1,999,999	● 250,000 - 499,999	⊕ 30,000 - 99,999	○ UNDER 10,000

SCALE 1:12,000,000   LAMBERT CONFORMAL CONIC PROJECTION

MILES   0   150   300   450

KILOMETERS   0   150   300   450

China, Japan, Korea, Mongolia

26

Southeastern Asia

Australia & New Zealand Comparisons

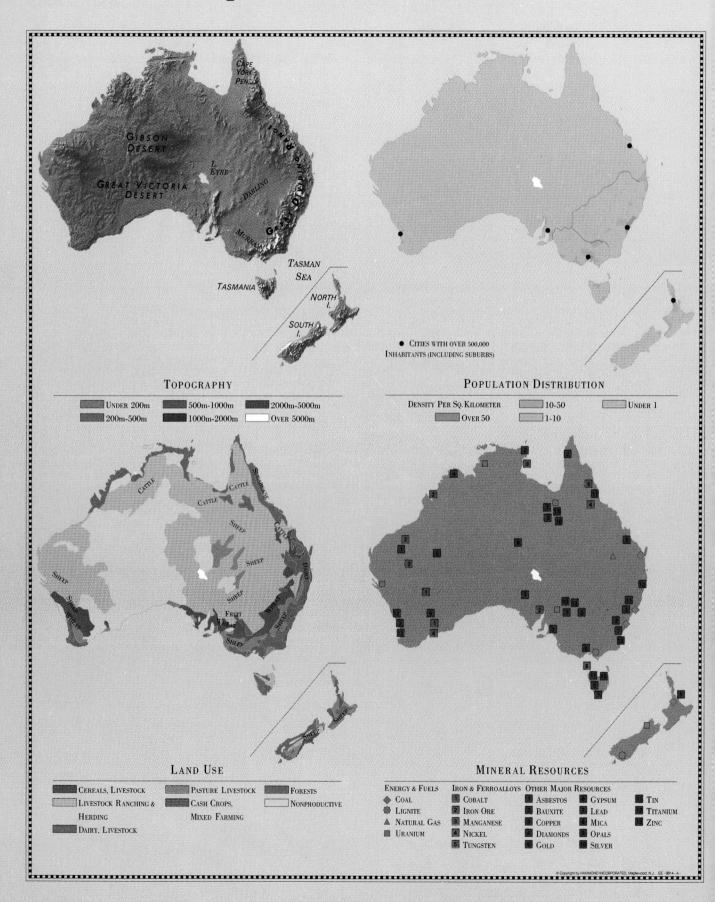

TOPOGRAPHY

- Under 200m
- 200m-500m
- 500m-1000m
- 1000m-2000m
- 2000m-5000m
- Over 5000m

POPULATION DISTRIBUTION

● Cities with over 500,000 Inhabitants (including suburbs)

Density Per Sq. Kilometer
- Over 50
- 10-50
- 1-10
- Under 1

LAND USE

- Cereals, Livestock
- Livestock Ranching & Herding
- Dairy, Livestock
- Pasture Livestock
- Cash Crops, Mixed Farming
- Forests
- Nonproductive

MINERAL RESOURCES

Energy & Fuels
- ◆ Coal
- ⬠ Lignite
- ▲ Natural Gas
- ■ Uranium

Iron & Ferroalloys
- 1 Cobalt
- 2 Iron Ore
- 3 Manganese
- 4 Nickel
- 5 Tungsten

Other Major Resources
- 6 Asbestos
- 7 Bauxite
- 8 Copper
- 9 Diamonds
- 10 Gold
- 11 Gypsum
- 12 Lead
- 13 Mica
- 14 Opals
- 15 Silver
- 16 Tin
- 17 Titanium
- 18 Zinc

Australia & New Zealand

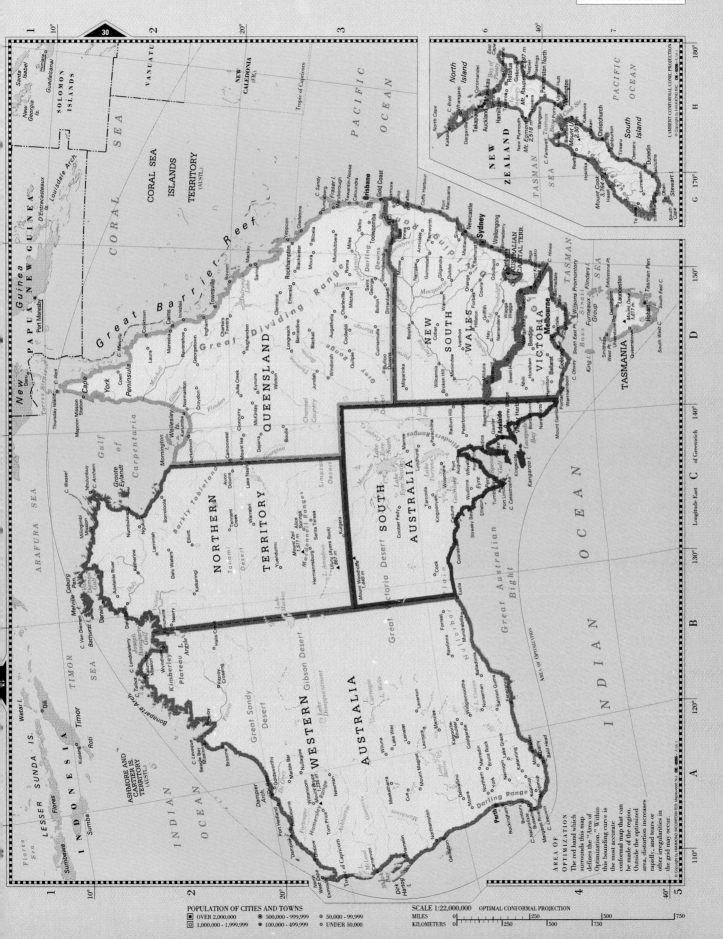

POPULATION OF CITIES AND TOWNS

■ OVER 2,000,000	● 500,000 - 999,999	● 50,000 - 99,999
▣ 1,000,000 - 1,999,999	● 100,000 - 499,999	○ UNDER 50,000

SCALE 1:22,000,000   OPTIMAL CONFORMAL PROJECTION

MILES   0   250   500   750

KILOMETERS   0   250   500   750

AREA OF OPTIMIZATION

The red band which surrounds this map defines the "Area of Optimization." Within this bounding curve is the most accurate conformal map that can be made of the region. Outside the optimized area, distortion increases rapidly, and tears or other irregularities in the grid may occur.

© Copyright by HAMMOND INCORPORATED, Maplewood, N.J.

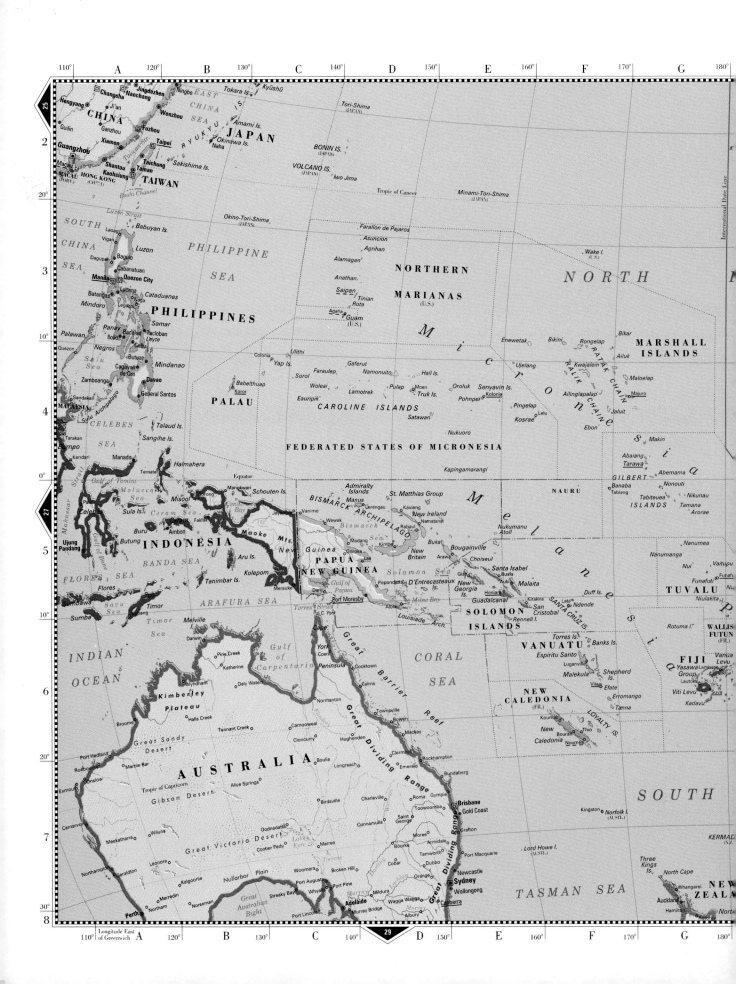

110° A 120° B 130° C 140° D 150° E 160° F 170° G 180°

CHINA
Changsha · Jingdezhen · Nanchang
Hengyang · Ji'an · Ningbo
Guilin · Ganzhou · Wenzhou
EAST CHINA SEA
Tokara Is. · Kyūshū
Amami Is.
Tori-Shima (JAPAN)

JAPAN
Guangzhou · Xiamen · Fuzhou
Macau · Taipei
MACAU (PORT.) · Shantou · Taichung
HONG KONG (CH'A) · Kaohsiung · Tainan
TAIWAN
Okinawa Is.
Naha
Sakishima Is.
BONIN IS. (JAPAN)

VOLCANO IS. (JAPAN)
Iwo Jima

Tropic of Cancer
Minami-Tori-Shima (JAPAN)

SOUTH CHINA SEA
Laoag · Babuyan Is.
Vigan · Luzon
Dagupan · Baguio
Manila · Quezon City
Batangas · Lucena
Mindoro · Naga · Legazpi

PHILIPPINE SEA

Okino-Tori-Shima (JAPAN)

Farallon de Pajaros
Asuncion
Agrihan
Alamagan
Anathan
NORTHERN MARIANAS (U.S.)
Saipan · Tinian · Rota
Agana · Guam (U.S.)

PHILIPPINES
Samar
Panay · Bacolod · Tacloban · Leyte
Palawan · Iloilo · Cebu
Quezon · Negros · Butuan
Zamboanga · Cagayan de Oro · Mindanao
Sandakan · Davao
MALAYSIA · General Santos
Sulu Archipelago
Tarakan · CELEBES SEA
Borneo · Talaud Is.
Kendari · Sangihe Is.
Manado · Ternate · Halmahera

Colonia · Ulithi
Yap Is. · Gaferut
Babelthuap · Sorol · Faraulep · Namonuito · Hall Is.
Koror · Woleai · Lamotrek · Pulap · Moen · Oroluk · Senyavin Is.
PALAU · Eauripik · Truk Is. · Pohnpei · Kolonia
CAROLINE ISLANDS
Satawan · Kosrae · Lelu
Nukuoro

Micronesia

Enewetak · Bikini · Rongelap · Bikar
Ujelang · Kwajalein · Ailuk
MARSHALL ISLANDS
Maloelap
Ailinglapalap · Majuro
Jaluit
Ebon

FEDERATED STATES OF MICRONESIA
Kapingamarangi

Makin · GILBERT ISLANDS
Abaiang · Tarawa · Abemama · Nonouti
Banaba · Tabiang · Tabiteuea · Nikunau · Tamana · Arorae
NAURU

INDONESIA
Equator
Ujung Pandang · Gulf of Tomini · Moluccan Sea
Celebes · Misool · Sorong · Manokwari · Schouten Is.
Sula Is. · Ceram Sea · Faktak · Jayapura · Vanimo
Makassar Strait · Buru · Ambon
Butung · Ceram Sea · Maoke Mts. · Wewak
PAPUA NEW GUINEA
Gulf of Bone · BANDA SEA · Aru Is. · New Guinea · Madang · Goroka · Lae
FLORES SEA · Tanimbar Is. · Kolepom · Daru · Popondetta
Sumbawa · Flores · Savu Sea · Timor · Merauke · Gulf of Papua · Port Moresby
Sumba · ARAFURA SEA · Torres Strait · C. York · Milne Bay

BISMARCK ARCHIPELAGO
Admiralty Islands · St. Matthias Group
Manus · Lorengau · Kavieng · New Ireland · Namatanai
New Guinea · Bismarck Sea · Rabaul
Kimbe · New Britain · Buka
Bougainville · Arawa
Choiseul · Solomon Sea
Santa Isabel
New Georgia Is. · Gizo · Buala · Malaita · Duff Is.
D'Entrecasteaux Is. · Auki · Honiara · Kirakira · Lata · Ndende
Guadalcanal · San Cristobal · SANTA CRUZ IS.
Louisiade Arch. · Rennell I.
SOLOMON ISLANDS

Melanesia
Nukumanu Atoll
Nanumea
Nanumanga
Nui · Vaitupu
TUVALU
Funafuti · Nukufetau
Niulakita

VANUATU
Torres Is. · Banks Is.
Espiritu Santo
Luganville · Shepherd Is.
Malekula · Vila · Efate
Erromango
Tanna

NEW CALEDONIA (FR.)
Koumac · New Caledonia · Bourail · Thio · LOYALTY IS.
Noumea

Rotuma I.
WALLIS FUTUN (FR.)
FIJI
Yasawa Group · Vanua Levu
Lautoka · Lambasa
Viti Levu · Suva
Kadavu

INDIAN OCEAN
Melville · Darwin
Pine Creek
Katherine · Daly Waters
Wyndham
Kimberley Plateau
Broome · Halls Creek
Great Sandy Desert
Port Hedland · Marble Bar
Roebourne · Tennant Creek
Onslow
Exmouth
Carnarvon · Meekatharra · Wiluna
Gulf of Carpentaria
York Peninsula · Coen · Cooktown
Cairns
Normanton
Camooweal
Cloncurry · Hughenden · Townsville
Bowen
Mackay
Great Dividing Range
Great Barrier Reef
CORAL SEA

SOUTH

AUSTRALIA
Tropic of Capricorn
Gibson Desert · Alice Springs
Northampton · Geraldton
Meekatharra · Wiluna
Leonora
Kalgoorlie
Merredin · Northam
Perth
Great Victoria Desert
Nullarbor Plain
Norseman
Great Australian Bight
Coober Pedy · Marree · Lake Eyre
Oodnadatta
Woomera · Port Augusta
Streaky Bay · Port Pirie
Port Lincoln · Whyalla
Adelaide · Murray Bridge
Birdsville · Boulia · Longreach · Clermont · Emerald · Rockhampton · Bundaberg
Charleville · Roma · Gympie
Cunnamulla · Saint George · Toowoomba · **Brisbane** · Gold Coast
Bourke · Moree · Grafton
Cobar · Tamworth · Armidale · Port Macquarie
Broken Hill · Dubbo · Orange
Mildura · Wagga Wagga · Newcastle
Wentworth · **Canberra** · **Sydney** · Wollongong
Albury

Kingston · Norfolk I. (AUSTL.)
Lord Howe I. (AUSTL.)

Three Kings Is.
North Cape · Whangarei · Auckland · **NEW ZEALAND**
Hamilton

TASMAN SEA

KERMADEC (N.Z.)

NORTH

110° A 120° B 130° C 140° 29 D 150° E 160° F 170° G 180°

Longitude East of Greenwich
International Date Line

Pacific Ocean, Philippines

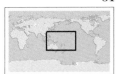

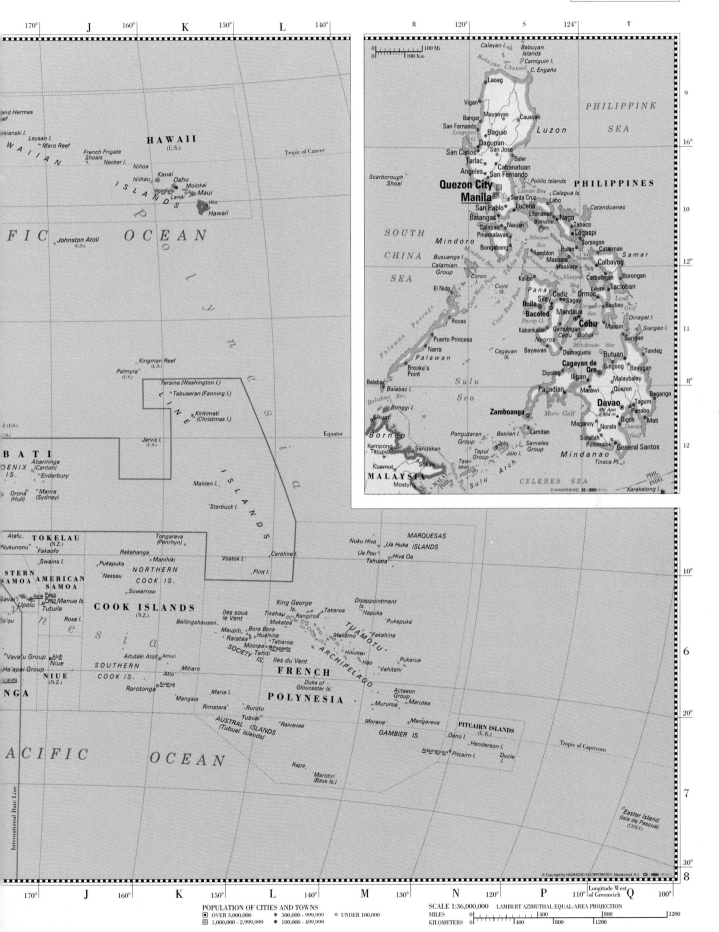

North America - Comparisons

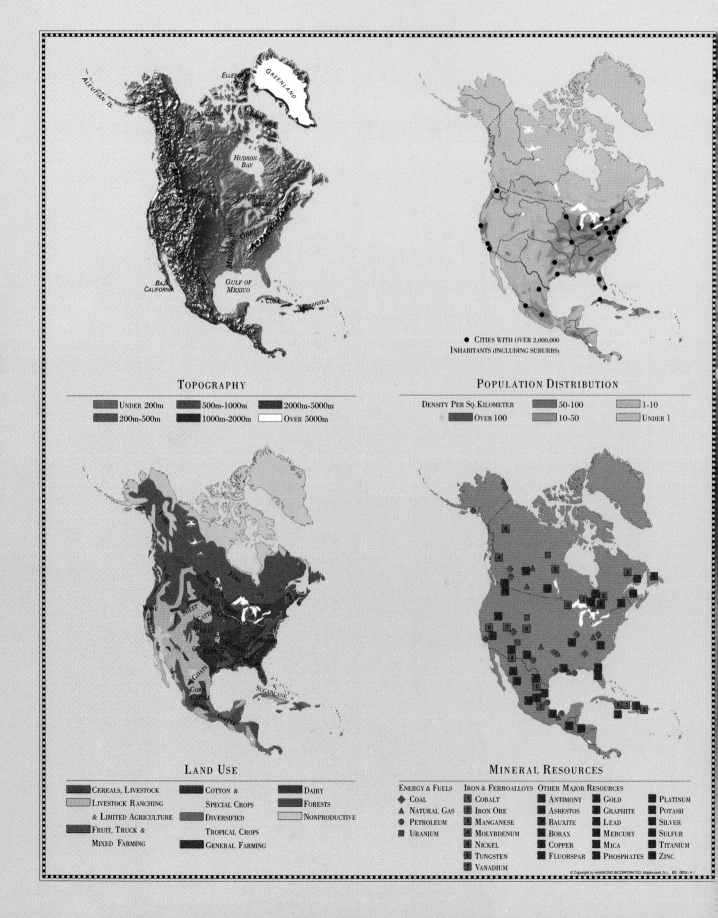

TOPOGRAPHY

UNDER 200m	500m-1000m	2000m-5000m
200m-500m	1000m-2000m	OVER 5000m

POPULATION DISTRIBUTION

● CITIES WITH OVER 2,000,000
INHABITANTS (INCLUDING SUBURBS)

DENSITY PER SQ. KILOMETER

	50-100	1-10
OVER 100	10-50	UNDER 1

LAND USE

CEREALS, LIVESTOCK	COTTON & SPECIAL CROPS	DAIRY
LIVESTOCK RANCHING & LIMITED AGRICULTURE	DIVERSIFIED	FORESTS
FRUIT, TRUCK & MIXED FARMING	TROPICAL CROPS	NONPRODUCTIVE
	GENERAL FARMING	

MINERAL RESOURCES

ENERGY & FUELS
◆ COAL
▲ NATURAL GAS
● PETROLEUM
■ URANIUM

IRON & FERROALLOYS
1 COBALT
2 IRON ORE
3 MANGANESE
4 MOLYBDENUM
5 NICKEL
6 TUNGSTEN
7 VANADIUM

OTHER MAJOR RESOURCES
ANTIMONY
ASBESTOS
BAUXITE
BORAX
COPPER
FLUORSPAR

GOLD
GRAPHITE
LEAD
MERCURY
MICA
PHOSPHATES

PLATINUM
POTASH
SILVER
SULFUR
TITANIUM
ZINC

© Copyright by HAMMOND INCORPORATED, Maplewood, N.J.   EE - 0015 - A

AREA OF OPTIMIZATION

The red band which surrounds this map defines the "Area of Optimization." Within this bounding curve is the most accurate conformal map that can be made of the region. Outside the optimized area, distortion increases rapidly, and tears or other irregularities in the grid may occur.

© Copyright by HAMMOND INCORPORATED, Maplewood, N.J.   CE-1076-A

SCALE 1:40,000,000   OPTIMAL CONFORMAL PROJECTION

MILES   0   500   1000   1500
KILOMETERS   0   500   1000   1500

POPULATION OF CITIES AND TOWNS

■ OVER 3,000,000   ▣ 500,000 - 999,999   ○ UNDER 100,000
▦ 1,000,000 - 2,999,999   ◉ 100,000 - 499,999

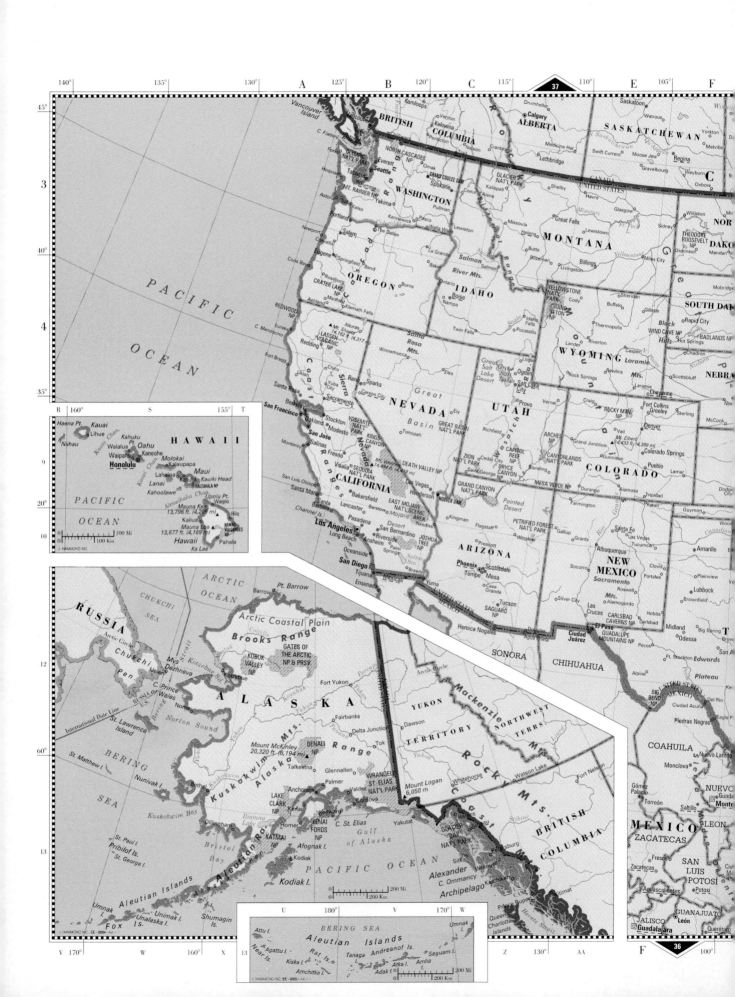

34

POPULATION OF CITIES AND TOWNS

■ OVER 2,000,000   ⊛ 500,000 - 999,999   ◉ 50,000 - 99,999
□ 1,000,000 - 1,999,999   ⊕ 100,000 - 499,999   ○ UNDER 50,000

SCALE 1:16,000,000   LAMBERT CONFORMAL CONIC PROJECTION

MILES   0   200   400   600
KILOMETERS   0   200   400   600

Mexico, Central America, West Indies

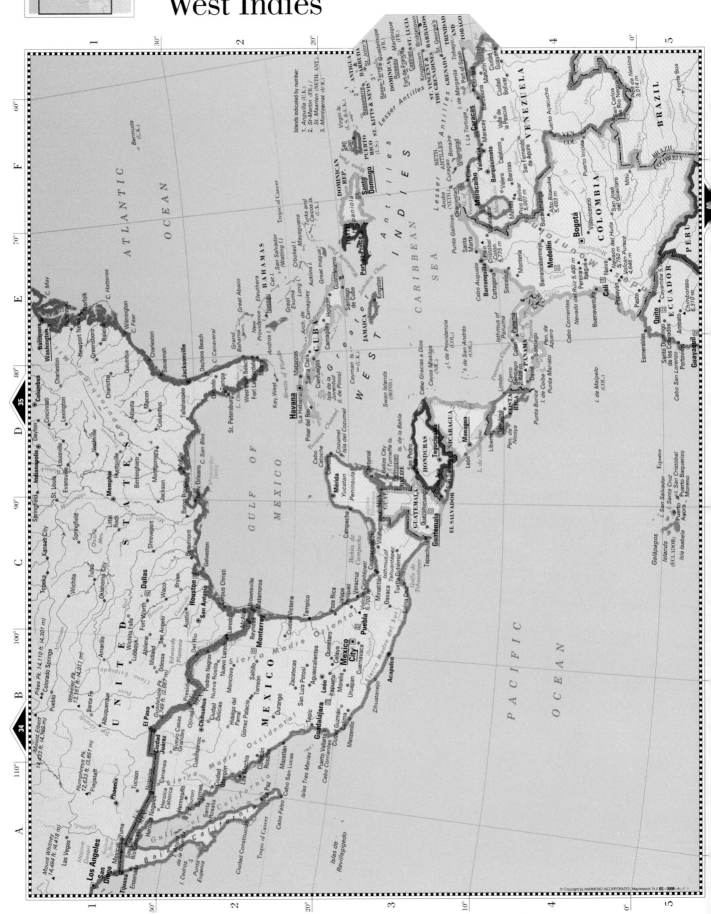

SCALE 1:26,000,000   LAMBERT CONFORMAL CONIC PROJECTION

MILES 0   300   600   900

KILOMETERS 0   300   600

POPULATION OF CITIES AND TOWNS

■ OVER 2,000,000	● 500,000 - 999,999	⊙ 50,000 - 99,999
▣ 1,000,000 - 1,999,999	◉ 100,000 - 499,999	○ UNDER 50,000

© Copyright by HAMMOND INCORPORATED, Maplewood, N.J. EE - 0006 - A A A

Canada

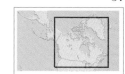

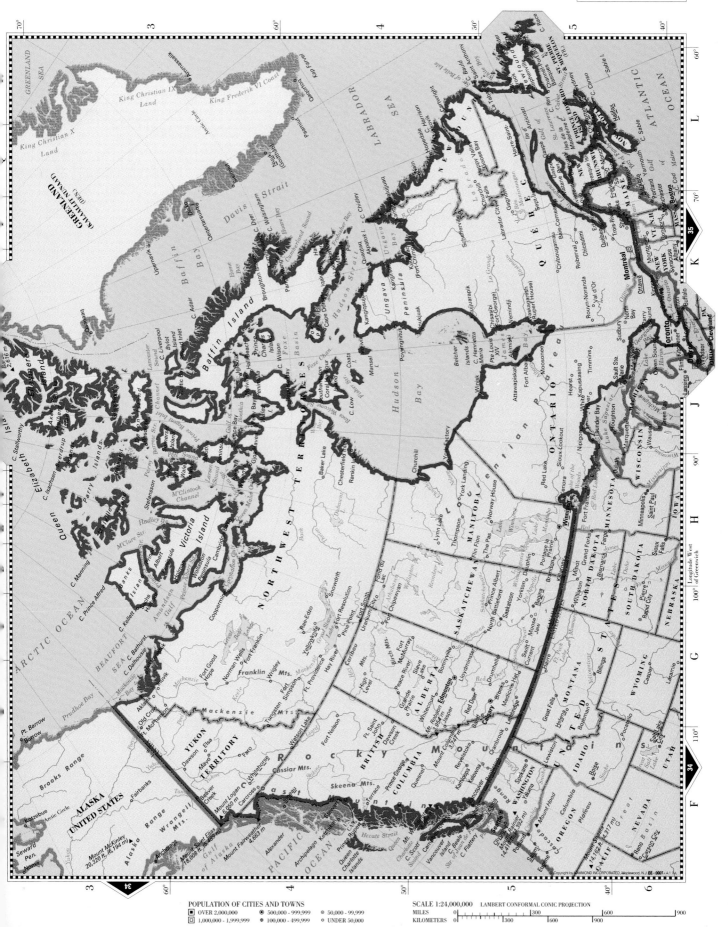

Arctic Regions, Antarctica

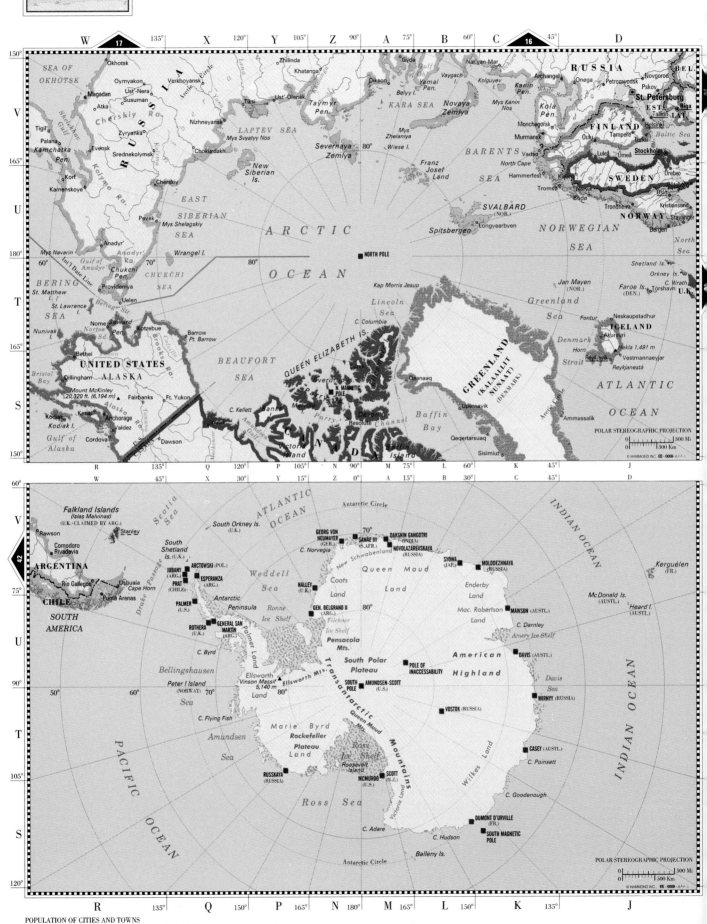

POPULATION OF CITIES AND TOWNS
- ■ OVER 2,000,000
- ⬓ 1,000,000 - 1,999,999
- ⦿ 500,000 - 999,999
- ⊙ 100,000 - 499,999
- ⦾ 50,000 - 99,999
- • UNDER 50,000

South America - Comparisons

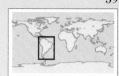

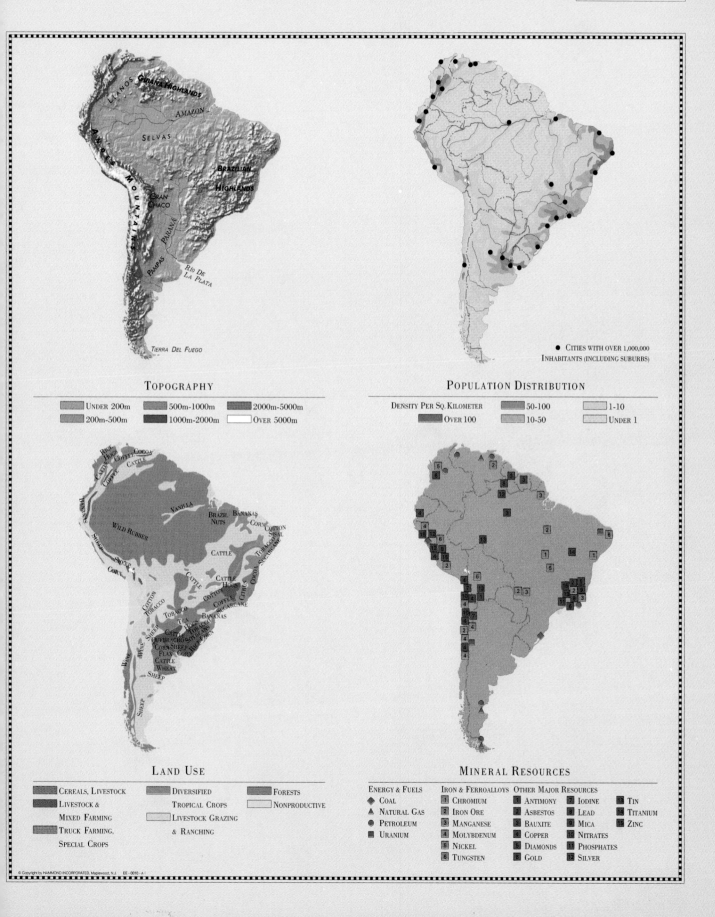

TOPOGRAPHY

Under 200m	500m-1000m	2000m-5000m
200m-500m	1000m-2000m	Over 5000m

POPULATION DISTRIBUTION

Density Per Sq. Kilometer

Over 100	50-100	1-10
	10-50	Under 1

● Cities with over 1,000,000 Inhabitants (including suburbs)

LAND USE

- Cereals, Livestock
- Livestock & Mixed Farming
- Truck Farming, Special Crops
- Diversified Tropical Crops
- Livestock Grazing & Ranching
- Forests
- Nonproductive

MINERAL RESOURCES

Energy & Fuels
- ◆ Coal
- ▲ Natural Gas
- ● Petroleum
- ■ Uranium

Iron & Ferroalloys
- 1 Chromium
- 2 Iron Ore
- 3 Manganese
- 4 Molybdenum
- 5 Nickel
- 6 Tungsten

Other Major Resources
- 1 Antimony
- 2 Asbestos
- 3 Bauxite
- 4 Copper
- 5 Diamonds
- 6 Gold
- 7 Iodine
- 8 Lead
- 9 Mica
- 10 Nitrates
- 11 Phosphates
- 12 Silver
- 13 Tin
- 14 Titanium
- 15 Zinc

POPULATION OF CITIES AND TOWNS

■ OVER 2,000,000	● 500,000 - 999,999
◙ 1,000,000 - 1,999,999	● 100,000 - 499,999
	◉ 50,000 - 99,999
	○ UNDER 50,000

SCALE 1:17,300,000   LAMBERT CONFORMAL CONIC PROJECTION

MILES   0   200   400   600

KILOMETERS   0   200   400   600

Southern South America

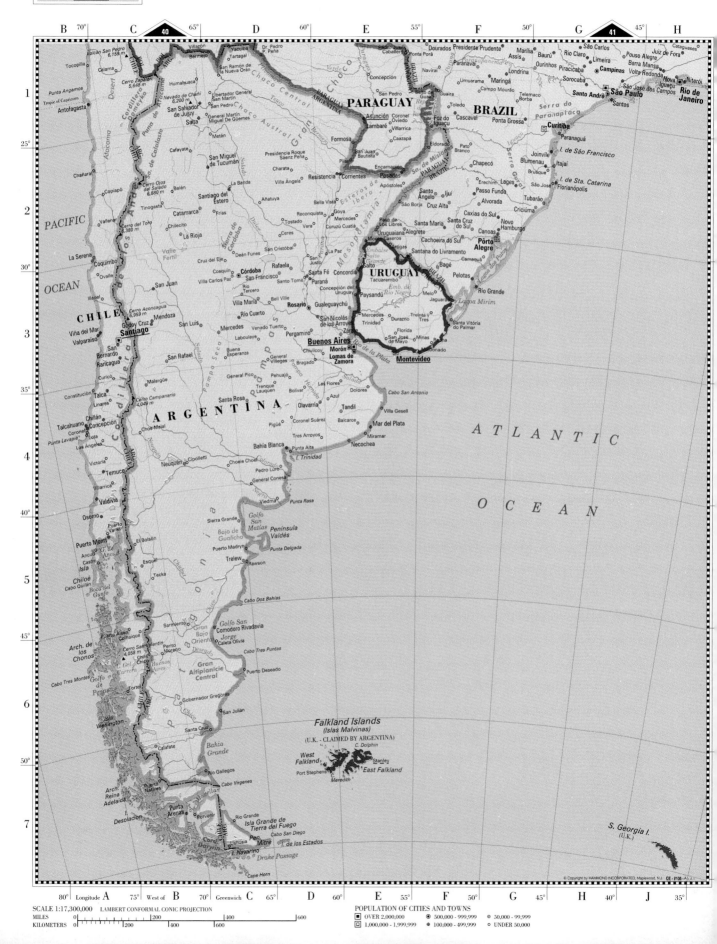

SCALE 1:17,300,000   LAMBERT CONFORMAL CONIC PROJECTION

MILES 0 ___ 200 ___ 400 ___ 600

KILOMETERS 0 ___ 200 ___ 400 ___ 600

POPULATION OF CITIES AND TOWNS

■ OVER 2,000,000	◉ 500,000 - 999,999	○ 50,000 - 99,999
▣ 1,000,000 - 1,999,999	◉ 100,000 - 499,999	○ UNDER 50,000

Africa - Comparisons

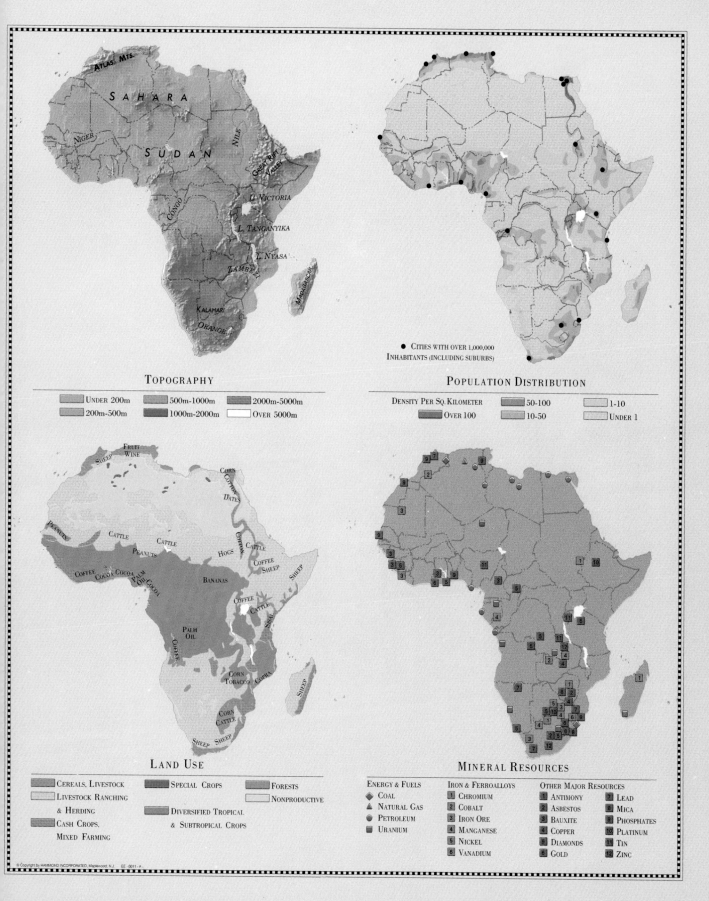

TOPOGRAPHY

ATLAS MTS.
SAHARA
NIGER
SUDAN
NILE
GREAT RIFT VALLEY
CONGO
L. VICTORIA
L. TANGANYIKA
L. NYASA
ZAMBEZI
MADAGASCAR
KALAHARI
ORANGE

UNDER 200m	500m-1000m	2000m-5000m
200m-500m	1000m-2000m	OVER 5000m

POPULATION DISTRIBUTION

● CITIES WITH OVER 1,000,000
INHABITANTS (INCLUDING SUBURBS)

DENSITY PER SQ. KILOMETER

	50-100	1-10
OVER 100	10-50	UNDER 1

LAND USE

FRUIT WINE
SHEEP
CORN
COTTON
DATES
PEANUTS
CATTLE
CATTLE
COTTON
CATTLE
PEANUTS
HOGS
COFFEE
COFFEE
COCOA COCOA
PALM OIL
COCOA
SHEEP
BANANAS
SHEEP
COFFEE
CATTLE
PALM OIL
SISAL
COFFEE
CORN
TOBACCO
COPRA
SHEEP
CORN
CATTLE
SHEEP SHEEP

CEREALS, LIVESTOCK	SPECIAL CROPS	FORESTS
LIVESTOCK RANCHING & HERDING		NONPRODUCTIVE
CASH CROPS, MIXED FARMING	DIVERSIFIED TROPICAL & SUBTROPICAL CROPS	

MINERAL RESOURCES

ENERGY & FUELS	IRON & FERROALLOYS	OTHER MAJOR RESOURCES	
◆ COAL	1 CHROMIUM	1 ANTIMONY	7 LEAD
▲ NATURAL GAS	2 COBALT	2 ASBESTOS	8 MICA
● PETROLEUM	3 IRON ORE	3 BAUXITE	9 PHOSPHATES
▢ URANIUM	4 MANGANESE	4 COPPER	10 PLATINUM
	5 NICKEL	5 DIAMONDS	11 TIN
	6 VANADIUM	6 GOLD	12 ZINC

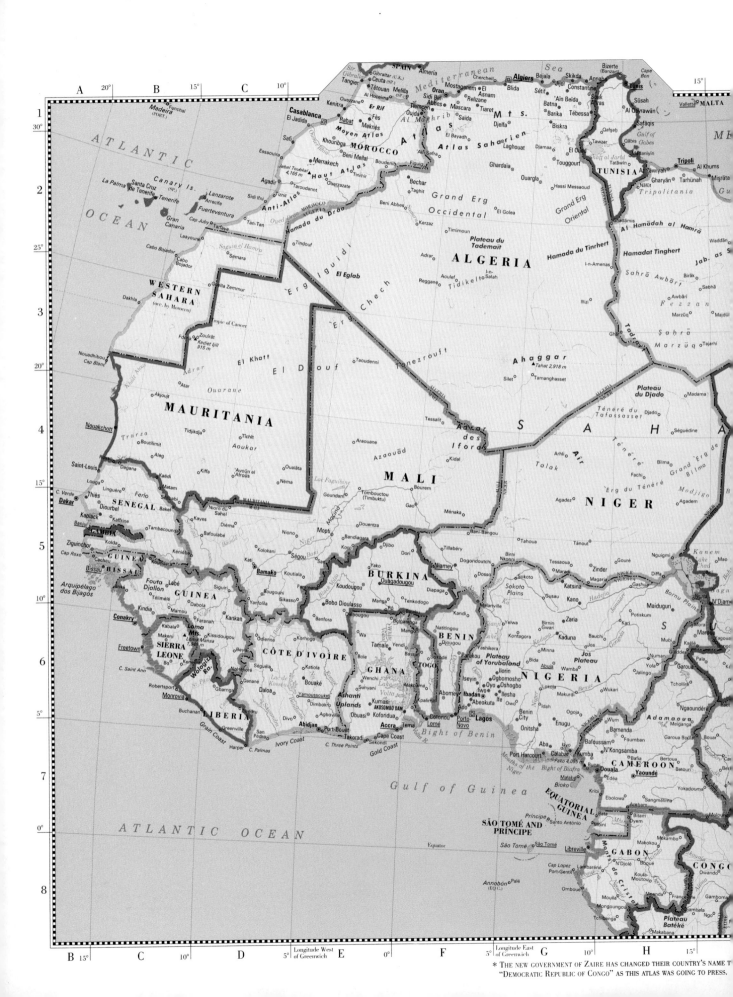

A 20° B 15° C 10°

ATLANTIC

OCEAN

Madeira
(PORT.)
Funchal

Canary Is.
La Palma
Santa Cruz
de Tenerife
Tenerife
Lanzarote
Arrecife
Fuerteventura
Gran
Canaria

Cabo Bojador
Cabo
Bojador

Nouadhibou
Cap Blanc

WESTERN
SAHARA
(occ. by Morocco)

Dakhla

Saguia el Hamra

Semara

Tindouf

'Erg Iguidi

El Eglab

Zouîrât
Kediet Ijill
915 m

Fdérik

Atar

Akjoujt

MAURITANIA

Tidjikdja

Tîchît

Aoukar

Boutilimit

Nouakchott

Aleg

Trarza

Saint-Louis

Dagana
Rosso

Louga
Linguère
Ferlo

Kaédi

Matam

Diéma

Kiffa

'Ayoûn el
Atroûs

Oualâta

Néma

Dakar
C. Verde
Thiès
Diourbel
Kaolack
Kaffrine
SENEGAL
Tambacounda
GAMBIA
Banjul
Ziguinchor
Cap Roxo
Cacheu
GUINEA
BISSAU
Bissau
Boké
Arquipélago
dos Bijagós
Bolama

Koundara
Fouta
Djallon
Labé
Kindia
Mamou
Dabola
Télimélé
Conakry
GUINEA
Kabala
Makeni
Freetown
SIERRA
LEONE
Bo
Kenema
C. Saint Ann
Robertsport
Monrovia
Buchanan
LIBERIA
Grain Coast
Greenville
Harper
C. Palmas

Siguiri
Kankan
Kissidougou
Faranah
Odienné
Beyla
Danané
Man
N'zérékoré
Loma
Mts.
Loma Mansa
1,948 m
Woloji
Ra.
St Paul

Séguéla

CÔTE D'IVOIRE

Katiola
Bouaké

Daloa

Lac de
Kossou

Yamoussoukro

Dimbokro

Agboville
Divo

San
Pédro

Abidjan
Port-Bouët
Ivory Coast
C. Three Points

MALI

Araouane

Tombouctou
(Timbuktu)

Goundam

Niafunké

Mopti

Douentza

Gao

Ménaka

Bourem

Lac Faguibine

Bandiagara

Djenné

Ségou
Koro
Djibo
Dori
Tillabéry
Niamey
Dosso
Tahoua
Tanout
Tessalit
Kidal
Adrar
des
Iforas
Azaouâd
BURKINA
Ouagadougou
Koudougou
Bobo Dioulasso
Banfora
Sikasso
Bougouni
Yanfolila
Manga
Tenkodogo
Diapaga
Kandi
Natitingou
BENIN
Djougou
Parakou
Bassar
Sokodé
Kara
TOGO
GHANA
Tamale
Yendi
Bole
Wa
Wenchi
Sunyani
Kumasi
AKOSOMBO DAM
Ashanti
Uplands
Obuasi
Kofondua
Koforidua
Accra
Tema
Cape Coast
Sekondi
Takoradi
Gold Coast
Volta R.
Lomé
Porto
Novo
Cotonou
Abomey
Lagos
Benin
City
Ibadan
Oyo
Ogbomosho
Ilesha
Ife
Oshogbo
Iseyin
Ilorin
Lokoja
Abuja
Minna
Kaduna
Zaria
Kano
Katsina
Gusau
Sokoto
Birnin
Kebbi
NIGERIA
Onitsha
Enugu
Benue
Makurdi
Ogoja
Jos
Plateau
Bauchi
Gombe
Yola
Jalingo
Wukari
Numan
Mubi
Maiduguri
Bornu Plain
Nguru
Potiskum
N'Djamena
Kukawa
Lake
Chad
Maradi
Zinder
Magaria
Gashua
Diffa
Nguigmi
Mao
Agadez
Arlit
'Erg du Ténéré
Fachi
Bilma
Modjigo
Adrar
NIGER
Talak
Aïr
Séguédine
Djado
Plateau
du Djado
Madama
Ténéré du
Tafassasset
Grand 'Erg de
Bilma

SAHARA

ALGERIA

Reggane

Tidikelt
I-n-
Salah
Aoulef

Adrar

Timimoun

Plateau du
Tademaït

Hamada du Tinrhert

Hamadat Tinghert

In-Amenas

Illizi

Ahaggar
Tahat 2,918 m

Silet

Tamanghasset

Sahrā
Marzūq

Tajarhī

Ghāt

Fezzan

Marzūq

Majdūl

Sabhā

Awbāri

Waddān

Birāk

Jab. as

Tanezrouft

'Erg Chech

Taoudenni

El Djouf

Ouarane

El Khatt

Adrar

Oualâta

Goulta Zemmur

Tropic of Cancer

Kerzaz

Beni Abbes

Taghit

Béchar

Grand Erg
Occidental

Grand Erg
Oriental

El Golea

Ghardaïa

Ouargla

Hassi Messaoud

Touggourt

El Oued

Djamaa

Laghouat

El Bayadh

'Aïn Sefra

Figuig

Bou-Denib

Aïn
Beni-Mathar

Oujda

Tlemcen

Mascara

Saïda

Tiaret

Relizane

El Asnam

Médéa

Blida

Algiers

Bejaïa

Jijel

Skikda

Annaba

Constantine

Sétif

Batna

Aïn Beïda

Tébessa

Biskra

El Kantara

Barika

Djelfa

Atlas Saharien

Laayoune

Tarfaya

Tan-Tan

Tiznit

Sidi Ifni

Anti-Atlas

Hamada du Dra'

Oued Dra'
MOROCCO
ALGERIA

Taroudannt

Agadir

Jebel Toubkal
4,165 m

Haut Atlas

Tinrhir

Ouarzazate

Marrakech

Essaouira

Safi

El Jadida

Casablanca

Rabat

Kenitra

Meknès

Fès

MOROCCO

Moyen Atlas

Khouribga

Beni Mellal

Boudenib

Al Hoceima

Tétouan
Ceuta (SP.)
Melilla
(SP.)
Tangier
Gibraltar (U.K.)

SPAIN

Almería

Cherchell

Mostaganem
Oran
Sidi Bel
Abbès

Bizerte
(Banzart)
Cape
Bon

Tunis

Sūsah

Safāqis

Qafṣah

Gafsa

Qābis
Gulf of
Gabes

TUNISIA

Tripolitania

Tripoli

Al Khums

Miṣrātah

Tarhūnah

Gharyān

Az Zawiyah

Ghadāmis

Al Hamādah al Hamrā

Waddān

Chott al Jarīd

Tatāwīn

Māniyīn

Nālūt

Valletta
MALTA

Mediterranean Sea

Er Rif

Al Maghrib

Atlas
Mts.

TUNISIA

20°
30°

1

2

25°

3

20°

4

15°

5

10°

6

5°

7

0°

8

ATLANTIC OCEAN

Gulf of Guinea

Equator

São Tomé
SÃO TOMÉ AND
PRÍNCIPE
Príncipe
Santo António
São Tomé
Annobón
(E.G.)
Palé

EQUATORIAL
GUINEA
Bata
Mbini
Kribi
Ebolowa
Bioko
Malabo
Douala
Yaoundé
CAMEROON
Bafia
Bertoua
Yokadouma
Sangmélima
Oyem
Bitam
Ambam
Makokou
Mékambo
Libreville
N'Djolé
Booué
GABON
Cap Lopez
Port-Gentil
Lambaréné
Koula-
Moutou
Omboué
Mouila
Tchibanga
Plateau
Batéké
Makabana
Mongoumbou
Bight of Biafra
Port Harcourt
Calabar
Kumba
Fako 4,095 m
Mamfé
N'Kongsamba
Bamenda
Foumban
Garoua Boulaï
Bouar
Ngaoundéré
Adamaoua
Meiganga
Garoua
Tcholliré
Kaélé
Maroua
Mbini
Mrts de Cristal
Ogooué

B 15° C 10° D 5° E 0° F 5° G 10° H 15°
Longitude West of Greenwich   Longitude East of Greenwich

* THE NEW GOVERNMENT OF ZAIRE HAS CHANGED THEIR COUNTRY'S NAME T[O]
"DEMOCRATIC REPUBLIC OF CONGO" AS THIS ATLAS WAS GOING TO PRESS.

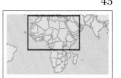

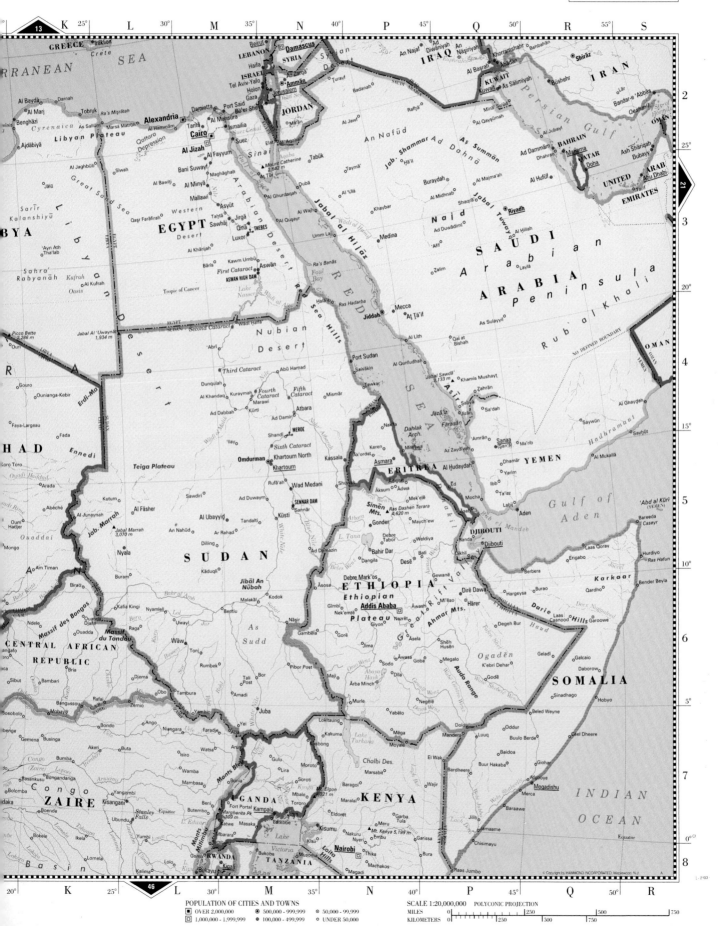

GREECE
Iráklion
Crete
MEDITERRANEAN SEA

LEBANON
Beirut
SYRIA
Damascus
Haifa
Az Zarqá
ISRAEL
Tel Aviv-Yafo
Amman
Holon
Jerusalem
JORDAN

IRAQ
An Najaf
Ad Dīwānīyah
An Nāṣirīyah
Khorramshahr
Behbahān
Shīrāz
Al Baṣrah
Abādān
IRAN
KUWAIT
Kuwait
As Sālimīyah
Būshehr
Bandar-e 'Abbās
Qeshm
Strait of Hormuz
OMAN

Al Baydā
Darnah
Al Marj
Tobruk
Ra's Miṣrātah
Benghāzi
Cyrenaica
Ajdābiyā
Libyan Plateau

Alexandria
Port Said
Damietta
Tanta
Al Manṣūrah
Al Hammām
Ismailia
Gaza
Be'er Sheva'
Suez
Cairo
Al Jīzah
Al Fayyūm
Beni Suwayf

Ad Dammān
BAHRAIN
Manama
Dhahran
QATAR
Doha
UNITED ARAB EMIRATES
Abu Dhabi
Ash Shāriqah
Dubayy

EGYPT
Western Desert
Asyūṭ
Sawhāj
Qinā
THEBES
Luxor
Nubian Desert

SAUDI ARABIA
Arabian Peninsula
Najd
Riyadh
Rub' al Khali
NO DEFINED BOUNDARY
OMAN

SUDAN

ETHIOPIA
Ethiopian Plateau
Addis Ababa

SOMALIA
Mogadishu
INDIAN OCEAN

ZAIRE
Congo (Zaïre)

GANDA
Kampala
RWANDA
Kigali
TANZANIA

KENYA
Nairobi

CENTRAL AFRICAN REPUBLIC

CHAD

© Copyright by HAMMOND INCORPORATED, Maplewood, N.J.

POPULATION OF CITIES AND TOWNS

- ■ OVER 2,000,000
- ▣ 1,000,000 - 1,999,999
- ⬤ 500,000 - 999,999
- ◉ 100,000 - 499,999
- ◎ 50,000 - 99,999
- ○ UNDER 50,000

SCALE 1:20,000,000   POLYCONIC PROJECTION

MILES   0   250   500   750
KILOMETERS   0   250   500   750

Southern Africa

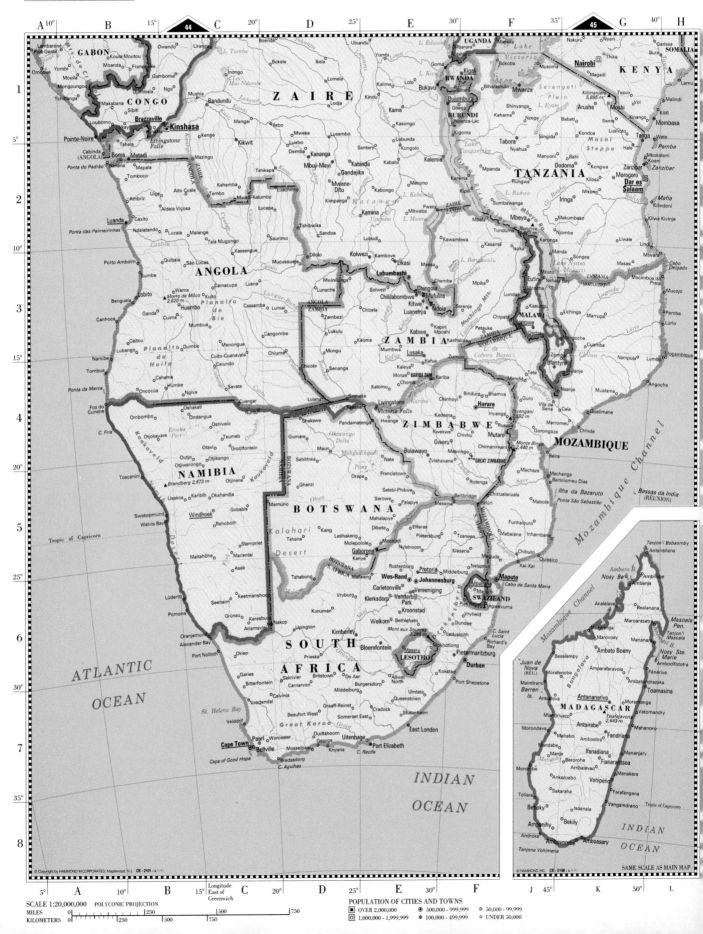

SCALE 1:20,000,000   POLYCONIC PROJECTION

MILES
KILOMETERS

POPULATION OF CITIES AND TOWNS
- ■ OVER 2,000,000
- ▣ 1,000,000 - 1,999,999
- ◉ 500,000 - 999,999
- ⊕ 100,000 - 499,999
- ⊙ 50,000 - 99,999
- ○ UNDER 50,000

SAME SCALE AS MAIN MAP

Index of the World

This index lists places and geographic features in the atlas including the country or area to which they belong. A page number and alpha-numeric reference appear in blue to the left of each entry. Capitals are designated by asterisks (*).

A
20/E2 **Abadan**, Iran
44/E6 **Abidjan**, Côte d'Ivoire
21/F4 **Abu Dhabi***, United Arab Emirates
44/G6 **Abuja***, Nigeria
36/C3 **Acapulco**, Mexico
44/E6 **Accra***, Ghana
42/B4 **Aconcagua** (mt.), Argentina
31/M7 **Adamstown***, Pitcairn
15/E6 **Adana**, Turkey
45/N6 **Addis Ababa***, Ethiopia
29/C4 **Adelaide**, Australia
45/Q5 **Aden** (gulf)
30/D5 **Admiralty** (isls.), Papua New Guinea
13/G2 **Adriatic** (sea), Europe
13/K4 **Aegean** (sea)
21/H2 **Afghanistan**
44 **Africa**
30/D3 **Agaña***, Guam
22/B3 **Ahmadabad**, India
20/E2 **Ahvaz**, Iran
35/J5 **Alabama** (state), U.S.
34/X12 **Alaska** (range), Alaska
34/X12 **Alaska** (state), U.S.
13/H3 **Albania**
35/M3 **Albany***, New York
20/E2 **Al Başrah**, Iraq
45/M7 **Albert** (lake), Africa
37/F4 **Alberta** (prov.), Canada
20/C1 **Aleppo**, Syria
34/W13 **Aleutian** (isls.), Alaska
45/L1 **Alexandria**, Egypt
44/F2 **Algeria**
44/F1 **Algiers***, Algeria
45/M2 **Al Jīzah**, Egypt
17/H5 **Almaty**, Kazakstan
12/E2 **Alps** (mts.), Europe
16/J5 **Altai** (mts.), Asia
24/E4 **Altun** (mts.), China
41/H4 **Amazon** (riv.), S. America
31/J6 **American Samoa**
20/C2 **Amman***, Jordan
21/K2 **Amritsar**, India
10/F3 **Amsterdam***, Netherlands
16/G5 **Amudar'ya** (riv.), Asia
38b/S **Amundsen** (sea), Antarctica
17/P4 **Amur** (riv.), Asia
15/C6 **Anatolia** (region), Turkey
34/Y12 **Anchorage**, Alaska
23/F5 **Andaman** (isls.), India
40/D6 **Andes** (mts.), S. America
12/D3 **Andorra**
12/D3 **Andorra la Vella***, Andorra
41/F2 **Angel** (falls), Venezuela
46/C3 **Angola**
15/D6 **Ankara***, Turkey
35/L4 **Annapolis***, Maryland
46/K10 **Antananarivo***, Madagascar
38b **Antarctica**
36/F3 **Antigua and Barbuda**
42/B1 **Antofagasta**, Chile
10/F4 **Antwerp**, Belgium
13/G3 **Apennines** (mts.), Italy
31/H6 **Apia***, W. Samoa
35/K4 **Appalachian** (mts.), U.S.
16/H4 **Aqmola***, Kazakstan
20/D4 **Arabian** (peninsula), Asia
21/H5 **Arabian** (sea), Asia
45/M2 **Arabian** (desert), Egypt
30/C5 **Arafura** (sea)
16/G5 **Aral** (sea), Asia
15/F6 **Ararat** (mt.), Turkey
38a **Arctic** (ocean)
42/C4 **Argentina**
14/D4 **Arhus**, Denmark
34/D5 **Arizona** (state), U.S.
35/H4 **Arkansas** (riv.), U.S.
35/H4 **Arkansas** (state), U.S.
15/F5 **Armenia**
40/D1 **Aruba** (Netherlands)
6/J6 **Ascension** (isl.), St. Helena
16/F6 **Ashgabat***, Turkmenistan
29/B2 **Ashmore and Cartier Isls.**, Australia
19 **Asia**
45/N4 **Asmara***, Eritrea
42/E2 **Asunción***, Paraguay
45/M3 **Aswân**, Egypt
42/C2 **Atacama** (desert), Chile
13/J4 **Athens***, Greece
35/K5 **Atlanta***, Georgia
6/G3 **Atlantic** (ocean)
44/E1 **Atlas** (mts.), Africa
29/H6 **Auckland**, New Zealand
35/N3 **Augusta***, Maine
35/G5 **Austin***, Texas
29 **Australia**
13/G2 **Austria**
15/G5 **Azerbaijan**
6/H4 **Azores** (isls.), Portugal
15/E4 **Azov** (sea), Europe

B
45/P5 **Bab el Mandeb** (strait)
37/J2 **Baffin** (isl.), N.W. Territories
20/D2 **Baghdad***, Iraq
36/E2 **Bahamas**
42/D4 **Bahia Blanca**, Argentina
20/F3 **Bahrain**
36/A2 **Baja California** (peninsula), Mexico
15/G5 **Baku***, Azerbaijan
12/D4 **Balearic** (isls.), Spain
26/D5 **Bali** (isl.), Indonesia
13/J3 **Balkan** (mts.), Europe
16/H5 **Balkhash** (lake), Kazakstan
11/J2 **Baltic** (sea), Europe
35/L4 **Baltimore**, Maryland
44/D5 **Bamako***, Mali
26/D3 **Bandar Seri Begawan***, Brunei
26/C5 **Bandung**, Indonesia
22/C5 **Bangalore**, India
23/H5 **Bangkok** (Krung Thep)*, Thailand
22/E3 **Bangladesh**
45/J7 **Bangui***, Central African Rep.
44/B5 **Banjul***, Gambia
36/F3 **Barbados**
12/D3 **Barcelona**, Spain
38a/D **Barents** (sea), Europe
13/H3 **Bari**, Italy
40/E1 **Barquisimeto**, Venezuela
40/D1 **Barranquilla**, Colombia
34/X11 **Barrow** (point), Alaska
29/D4 **Bass** (strait), Australia
36/F3 **Basse-Terre***, Guadeloupe
36/F3 **Basseterre***, St. Kitts & Nevis
35/H5 **Baton Rouge***, Louisiana
17/L4 **Baykal** (lake), Russia
38a/R **Beaufort** (sea), N. America
25/L4 **Beijing** (Peking)*, China
20/C2 **Beirut***, Lebanon
11/L3 **Belarus**
41/J4 **Belém**, Brazil
10/C3 **Belfast***, N. Ireland
10/E4 **Belgium**
13/J2 **Belgrade***, Yugoslavia
36/D3 **Belize**
36/D3 **Belmopan***, Belize
41/K8 **Belo Horizonte**, Brazil
23/E4 **Bengal** (bay), Asia
44/F5 **Benin**
44/G6 **Benue** (riv.), Nigeria
14/C3 **Bergen**, Norway
17/T4 **Bering** (sea)
34/W13 **Bering** (strait)
11/H3 **Berlin***, Germany
36/F1 **Bermuda**
12/E2 **Bern***, Switzerland
22/C3 **Bhopal**, India
22/E2 **Bhutan**
10/D3 **Birmingham**, England
12/B2 **Biscay** (bay), Europe
16/H5 **Bishkek***, Kyrgyzstan
34/F2 **Bismarck***, N. Dakota
44/B5 **Bissau***, Guinea-Bissau
15/D5 **Black** (sea)
10/G5 **Black** (forest), Germany
34/F3 **Black Hills** (mts.), U.S.
12/E2 **Blanc** (mt.), Europe
45/M5 **Blue Nile** (riv.), Africa
40/D3 **Bogotá***, Colombia
10/H4 **Bohemia** (region), Czech Rep.
34/C3 **Boise***, Idaho
40/F7 **Bolivia**
13/F2 **Bologna**, Italy
22/B4 **Bombay**, India
40/E1 **Bonaire** (isl.), Neth. Antilles
30/D2 **Bonin** (isls.), Japan
10/F4 **Bonn**, Germany
12/C2 **Bordeaux**, France
27/E3 **Borneo** (isl.), Asia
14/E5 **Bornholm** (isl.), Denmark
13/H2 **Bosnia and Herzegovina**
35/M3 **Boston***, Massachusetts
14/F3 **Bothnia** (gulf), Europe
46/D5 **Botswana**
23/F2 **Brahmaputra** (riv.), Asia
41/J7 **Brasilia***, Brazil
13/K2 **Braşov**, Romania
11/H1 **Bratislava***, Slovakia
40/F5 **Brazil**
46/C1 **Brazzaville***, Congo
10/G3 **Bremen**, Germany
11/K3 **Brest**, Belarus
12/B1 **Brest**, France
29/E3 **Brisbane**, Australia
10/C4 **Bristol** (channel), U.K.
37/E4 **British Columbia** (prov.), Canada
19/G10 **British Indian Ocean Territory**
11/J4 **Brno**, Czech Rep.
26/D2 **Brunei**
10/F4 **Brussels***, Belgium
13/K2 **Bucharest***, Romania
13/H2 **Budapest***, Hungary
42/E3 **Buenos Aires***, Argentina
46/E1 **Bujumbura***, Burundi
13/K3 **Bulgaria**
44/E5 **Burkina**
23/G3 **Burma** (Myanmar)
46/E1 **Burundi**

C
46/B2 **Cabinda**, Angola
37/L5 **Cabot** (strait), Canada
12/B4 **Cádiz** (gulf), Europe
45/M1 **Cairo***, Egypt
22/E3 **Calcutta**, India
37/F4 **Calgary**, Alberta
40/C3 **Cali**, Colombia
34/C4 **California** (state), U.S.
36/A2 **California** (gulf), Mexico
23/H5 **Cambodia**
44/H7 **Cameroon**
36/C3 **Campeche** (bay), Mexico
37 **Canada**
44/B2 **Canary** (isls.), Spain
29/D4 **Canberra***, Australia
25/K7 **Canton** (Guangzhou), China
46/C7 **Cape Town***, S. Africa
6/H5 **Cape Verde**
40/E1 **Caracas***, Venezuela
10/D4 **Cardiff***, Wales
36/E3 **Caribbean** (sea)
30/D4 **Caroline** (isls.), Micronesia
11/J4 **Carpathians** (mts.), Europe
29/C2 **Carpentaria** (gulf), Australia
34/C4 **Carson City***, Nevada
40/C1 **Cartagena**, Colombia
44/D1 **Casablanca**, Morocco
34/B3 **Cascade** (range), U.S.
16/F6 **Caspian** (sea)
36/F3 **Castries***, St. Lucia
12/D3 **Catalonia** (region), Spain
15/F5 **Caucasus** (mts.)
41/H3 **Cayenne***, Fr. Guiana
36/D3 **Cayman Islands** (U.K.)
31/S11 **Cebu**, Philippines
27/F3 **Celebes** (sea), Asia
27/E4 **Celebes** (isl.), Indonesia
10/C4 **Celtic** (sea), Europe
45/J6 **Central African Rep.**
45/J4 **Chad**
44/H5 **Chad** (lake), Africa
25/L5 **Chang Jiang** (Yangtze) (riv.), China
25/K6 **Changsha**, China
10/D4 **Channel Islands**, U.K.
35/K4 **Charleston***, W. Virginia
37/L5 **Charlottetown***, Prince Edward Isl.
16/G4 **Chelyabinsk**, Russia
35/L4 **Chesapeake** (bay), U.S.
34/F3 **Cheyenne***, Wyoming
35/J3 **Chicago**, Illinois
36/B2 **Chihuahua**, Mexico
42/B3 **Chile**
40/C4 **Chimborazo** (mt.), Ecuador
24/G5 **China**
13/L2 **Chişinău***, Moldova
23/F3 **Chittagong**, Bangladesh
24/J6 **Chongqing** (Chungking), China
38a/T **Chukchi** (sea)
35/K4 **Cincinnati**, Ohio
36/B1 **Ciudad Juárez**, Mexico
35/K3 **Cleveland**, Ohio
13/J2 **Cluj-Napoca**, Romania
37/D3 **Coast** (mts.), Canada
34/B4 **Coast** (ranges), U.S.
22/C6 **Cochin**, India
10/F4 **Cologne** (Köln), Germany
40/D3 **Colombia**
22/C6 **Colombo***, Sri Lanka
34/D5 **Colorado** (riv.), N. America
34/E4 **Colorado** (state), U.S.
37/E5 **Columbia** (riv.), N. America
35/K5 **Columbia***, S. Carolina
35/K4 **Columbus***, Ohio
7/M6 **Comoros**
44/C6 **Conakry***, Guinea
42/B4 **Concepción**, Chile
35/M3 **Concord***, New Hampshire
44/H8 **Congo**
46/C1 **Congo** (riv.), Africa
35/M3 **Connecticut** (state), U.S.
10/G5 **Constance** (lake), Europe
31/J6 **Cook Islands**, New Zealand
11/H3 **Copenhagen***, Denmark
30/E6 **Coral** (sea)
42/D3 **Córdoba**, Argentina
12/B4 **Córdoba**, Spain
13/H4 **Corfu** (Kérkira), Greece
13/F3 **Corsica** (isl.), France
36/D4 **Costa Rica**
44/D6 **Côte d'Ivoire**
13/K5 **Crete** (isl.), Greece
15/D4 **Crimea** (peninsula), Ukraine
13/G2 **Croatia**
36/E2 **Cuba**
40/E1 **Curaçao** (isl.), Neth. Antilles
42/G2 **Curitiba**, Brazil
13/K4 **Cyclades** (isls.), Greece
20/B1 **Cyprus**
11/H4 **Czech Republic**

D
44/B5 **Dakar***, Senegal
34/D5 **Dallas**, Texas
20/C2 **Damascus***, Syria
23/J4 **Da Nang**, Vietnam
13/L2 **Danube** (riv.), Europe
13/K4 **Dardanelles** (strait), Turkey
46/G2 **Dar es Salaam***, Tanzania
29/D4 **Darling** (riv.), Australia
31/T12 **Davao**, Philippines
20/C2 **Dead** (sea), Asia
35/L4 **Delaware** (state), U.S.
22/C2 **Delhi**, India
10/G3 **Denmark**
34/E4 **Denver***, Colorado
35/H3 **Des Moines***, Iowa
34/K3 **Detroit**, Michigan
22/E3 **Dhaka (Dacca)***, Bangladesh
45/P5 **Djibouti**
45/P5 **Djibouti***, Djibouti
15/D4 **Dnepr (Dnieper)** (riv.), Europe
20/F3 **Doha***, Qatar
36/F3 **Dominica**
36/F3 **Dominican Republic**
15/F4 **Don** (riv.), Russia
15/E4 **Donets'k**, Ukraine
10/F4 **Dortmund**, Germany
44/G7 **Douala**, Cameroon
10/C3 **Douglas***, Isle of Man
10/E4 **Dover** (strait), Europe
35/L4 **Dover***, Delaware
38b/V **Drake** (passage)
46/E6 **Drakensburg** (mts.), S. Africa
11/H4 **Dresden**, Germany
10/C3 **Dublin***, Ireland
46/F6 **Durban**, S. Africa
16/G6 **Dushanbe***, Tajikistan
10/F4 **Düsseldorf**, Germany

E
25/M6 **East China** (sea), Asia
31/Q7 **Easter** (isl.), Chile
40/C4 **Ecuador**
10/D3 **Edinburgh***, Scotland
37/F4 **Edmonton***, Alberta
45/L2 **Egypt**
13/F3 **Elba** (isl.), Italy
15/F5 **El'brus** (mt.), Russia
20/E1 **Elburz** (mts.), Iran
37/J2 **Ellesmere** (isl.), N.W. Territories
36/C3 **El Salvador**
10/D3 **England**, U.K.
10/C4 **English** (channel), Europe
44/G7 **Equatorial Guinea**
35/K3 **Erie** (lake), N. America
45/N5 **Eritrea**
20/F2 **Esfahān**, Iran
10/F4 **Essen**, Germany
11/L2 **Estonia**
45/N5 **Ethiopia**
20/D2 **Euphrates** (riv.), Asia
9 **Europe**
22/E2 **Everest** (mt.), Asia
13/K4 **Évvoia** (isl.), Greece
29/C3 **Eyre** (lake), Australia

F
21/K2 **Faisalabad**, Pakistan
42/D7 **Falkland Islands**, U.K.
9/D2 **Faroe** (isls.), Denmark
30/G6 **Fiji**
14/H2 **Finland**
14/H4 **Finland** (gulf), Europe
13/F3 **Florence** (Firenze), Italy
35/K6 **Florida** (state), U.S.
41/L4 **Fortaleza**, Brazil
36/F3 **Fort-de-France***, Martinique
12/D2 **France**
35/K4 **Frankfort***, Kentucky
10/G4 **Frankfurt am Main**, Germany
37/L5 **Fredericton***, New Brunswick
44/C6 **Freetown***, Sierra Leone
41/H3 **French Guiana**
31/M6 **French Polynesia**
25/P5 **Fukuoka**, Japan
30/G5 **Funafuti***, Tuvalu
37/L5 **Fundy** (bay), N. America

G
44/H7 **Gabon**
46/E5 **Gaborone***, Botswana
6/E6 **Galápagos** (isls.), Ecuador
44/B5 **Gambia**
22/E3 **Ganges** (riv.), Asia
20/B2 **Gaza**, Gaza Strip
11/J3 **Gdańsk** (gulf), Poland
12/E2 **Geneva**, Switzerland
13/F2 **Genoa** (Genova), Italy
41/G2 **Georgetown***, Guyana
15/F5 **Georgia**
35/K5 **Georgia** (state), U.S.
10/G4 **Germany**
44/E6 **Ghana**
12/B4 **Gibraltar**, U.K.
30/G5 **Gilbert Isls.**, Kiribati
10/C3 **Glasgow**, Scotland
41/J7 **Goânia**, Brazil
24/H3 **Gobi** (desert), Asia
33/M3 **Godthåb (Nuuk)***, Greenland
46/C7 **Good Hope** (cape), S. Africa
14/D4 **Göteborg**, Sweden
14/F4 **Gotland** (isl.), Sweden
12/C4 **Granada**, Spain
35/G6 **Grande, Rio** (riv.), N. America
10/D2 **Great Britain** (isl.), U.K.
29/D4 **Great Dividing** (range), Australia
34/D3 **Great Salt** (lake), Utah
29/B2 **Great Sandy** (desert), Australia
29/B3 **Great Victoria** (desert), Australia
25/K4 **Great Wall**, China
13/J4 **Greece**
33/N2 **Greenland**, Denmark
36/F3 **Grenada**
36/B2 **Guadalajara**, Mexico
12/B4 **Guadalquivir** (riv.), Spain
36/F3 **Guadeloupe** (France)
30/D3 **Guam**, U.S.
25/K7 **Guangzhou**, China
36/E3 **Guantánamo**, Cuba
36/C3 **Guatemala**
36/C3 **Guatemala***, Guatemala
40/B4 **Guayaquil**, Ecuador
44/C5 **Guinea**
44/F7 **Guinea** (gulf), Africa
44/B5 **Guinea-Bissau**
40/G3 **Guyana**
22/C2 **Gwalior**, India

H
10/F3 **Hague, The***, Netherlands
23/J4 **Hainan** (isl.), China
23/J3 **Haiphong**, Vietnam
36/E3 **Haiti**
37/L5 **Halifax***, Nova Scotia
10/G3 **Hamburg**, Germany
37/J5 **Hamilton**, Ontario
10/G3 **Hannover**, Germany
23/J3 **Hanoi***, Vietnam
46/E4 **Harare***, Zimbabwe
25/N2 **Harbin**, China
35/L3 **Harrisburg***, Pennsylvania
35/M3 **Hartford***, Connecticut
36/D2 **Havana***, Cuba
34/S9 **Hawaii** (state), U.S.
10/B2 **Hebrides, Outer** (isls.), Scotland
34/D2 **Helena***, Montana
14/H3 **Helsinki***, Finland
24/E6 **Himalaya** (mts.), Asia
21/J1 **Hindu Kush** (mts.), Asia
25/P5 **Hiroshima**, Japan
36/E3 **Hispaniola** (isl.), W. Indies
29/D5 **Hobart**, Australia
23/J5 **Ho Chi Minh City** (Saigon), Vietnam
25/R3 **Hokkaidō** (isl.), Japan
11/M3 **Homyel'**, Belarus
36/D3 **Honduras**
25/K7 **Hong Kong**, China
34/S9 **Honolulu***, Hawaii
25/Q5 **Honshu** (isl.), Japan
21/G3 **Hormuz** (strait), Asia
42/C8 **Horn** (cape), Chile
34/G6 **Houston**, Texas
25/L4 **Huang He** (Yellow) (riv.), China
37/J3 **Hudson** (bay), Canada
13/H2 **Hungary**
35/K2 **Huron** (lake), N. America
20/C4 **Hyderabad**, India
21/J3 **Hyderabad**, Pakistan

I
44/F6 **Ibadan**, Nigeria
12/D4 **Ibiza** (isl.), Spain
14/N7 **Iceland**
34/C3 **Idaho** (state), U.S.
35/H4 **Illinois** (state), U.S.
25/N4 **Inch'ŏn**, S. Korea
19/G7 **India**
7/N6 **Indian** (ocean)
35/J4 **Indiana** (state), U.S.
35/J4 **Indianapolis***, Indiana
23/H4 **Indochina** (region), Asia
27/E4 **Indonesia**
21/J4 **Indus** (riv.), Asia
25/K3 **Inner Mongolia** (region), China
13/F2 **Innsbruck**, Austria
13/H4 **Ionian** (isls.), Greece
34/H3 **Iowa** (state), U.S.
19/E6 **Iran**
20/D2 **Iraq**
10/B3 **Ireland**
10/C3 **Ireland, Northern**, U.K.
27/J4 **Irian Jaya** (region), Indonesia
10/C3 **Irish** (sea), Europe
17/L4 **Irkutsk**, Russia
23/G4 **Irrawaddy** (riv.), Myanmar
21/K2 **Islamabad***, Pakistan
10/C3 **Isle of Man**, U.K.
20/B2 **Israel**
15/C5 **Istanbul**, Turkey
13/F3 **Italy**
44/D6 **Ivory Coast** (Côte d'Ivoire)
30/D2 **Iwo Jima** (isl.), Japan
15/H2 **Izhevsk**, Russia
15/C6 **Izmir**, Turkey

J
35/H5 **Jackson***, Mississippi
22/C2 **Jaipur**, India
26/C5 **Jakarta***, Indonesia
36/E3 **Jamaica**
9/D1 **Jan Mayen** (isl.), Norway
25/Q4 **Japan**
25/P4 **Japan** (sea), Asia
26/C5 **Java** (isl.), Indonesia
26/D5 **Java** (sea), Indonesia
35/H4 **Jefferson City***, Missouri
20/C2 **Jerusalem***, Israel
20/C4 **Jiddah**, Saudi Arabia
46/E6 **Johannesburg**, S. Africa
20/C2 **Jordan**

34/Z13 Juneau*, Alaska
12/E2 Jura (mts.), Europe

K
21/J2 Kabul*, Afghanistan
46/D5 Kalahari (desert), Africa
11/K3 Kaliningrad, Russia
45/M7 Kampala*, Uganda
22/D2 Kānpur, India
35/G4 Kansas (state), U.S.
35/H4 Kansas City, Missouri
38a/A Kara (sea), Russia
21/J4 Karachi, Pakistan
46/C2 Katanga (region), Zaire
22/E2 Kathmandu*, Nepal
16/G5 Kazakstan
15/G2 Kazan', Russia
35/J4 Kentucky (state), U.S.
45/N7 Kenya
30/G8 Kermadec (isls.), New Zealand
15/E3 Kharkiv, Ukraine
45/M4 Khartoum*, Sudan
15/D3 Kiev* (Kyïv), Ukraine
46/F1 Kigali*, Rwanda
46/G1 Kilimanjaro (mt.), Tanzania
36/E3 Kingston*, Jamaica
36/F3 Kingstown*, St. Vincent & Grenadines
46/C1 Kinshasa*, Zaire
30/H5 Kiribati
25/P5 Kitakyushu, Japan
25/Q5 Kobe, Japan
30/E4 Kolonia*, Micronesia
25/N3 Korea, North
25/N4 Korea, South
30/C4 Koror*, Palau
11/J4 Kraków, Poland
26/B3 Kuala Lumpur*, Malaysia
20/D1 Kurdistan (region), Asia
17/P5 Kuril (isls.), Russia
20/E3 Kuwait
20/E3 Kuwait*, Kuwait
25/Q4 Kyoto, Japan
16/H5 Kyrgyzstan
25/P5 Kyushu (isl.), Japan

L
37/M4 Labrador (sea), N. America
44/F6 Lagos, Nigeria
21/K2 Lahore, Pakistan
35/K3 Lansing*, Michigan
23/H3 Laos
40/E7 La Paz*, Bolivia
11/L2 Latvia
20/C2 Lebanon
10/D3 Leeds, England
11/H4 Leipzig, Germany
17/N3 Lena (riv.), Russia
36/B2 León, Mexico
46/E6 Lesotho
24/D6 Lhasa, China
44/D6 Liberia
46/G7 Libreville*, Gabon
45/J2 Libya
45/K2 Libyan (desert), Africa
13/F2 Liechtenstein
40/C6 Lima*, Peru
35/G3 Lincoln*, Nebraska
12/A4 Lisbon*, Portugal
11/K3 Lithuania
35/H5 Little Rock*, Arkansas
10/D3 Liverpool, England
13/G2 Ljubljana*, Slovenia
40/D3 Llanos (plain), S. America
12/C2 Loire (riv.), France
44/F6 Lomé*, Togo
10/D4 London*, U.K.
34/C5 Los Angeles, California
35/H5 Louisiana (state), U.S.
46/B2 Luanda*, Angola
13/F2 Lucerne (Luzern), Switzerland
22/D2 Lucknow, India
46/E4 Lusaka*, Zambia
10/F4 Luxembourg
10/F4 Luxembourg*, Luxembourg
31/S9 Luzon (isl.), Philippines
15/B4 Lviv (L'vov), Ukraine
12/E2 Lyon, France

M
25/K7 Macau, Portugal
13/J3 Macedonia
37/M3 Mackenzie (riv.), Canada
46/K10 Madagascar
44/B1 Madeira (isl.), Portugal
35/J3 Madison*, Wisconsin
20/D5 Madras, India
12/C3 Madrid*, Spain
40/D3 Magdalena (riv.), Colombia
42/B7 Magellan (strait), S. America
35/N2 Maine (state), U.S.
12/D3 Majorca (isl.), Spain
31/G4 Majuro*, Marshall Isls.
44/G7 Malabo*, Equatorial Guinea
26/A2 Malacca (strait), Asia
46/F3 Malawi
26/C2 Malaysia
19/G9 Maldives
19/G9 Male*, Maldives
44/E4 Mali

14/C5 Malmö, Sweden
13/G5 Malta
36/D3 Managua*, Nicaragua
20/F3 Manama*, Bahrain
40/F4 Manaus, Brazil
25/M3 Manchuria (region), China
23/G3 Mandalay, Myanmar
45/P5 Mandeb, Bab el (strait)
31/S10 Manila*, Philippines
37/H4 Manitoba (prov.), Canada
46/F6 Maputo*, Mozambique
40/D1 Maracaibo, Venezuela
15/E4 Mariupol', Ukraine
15/C5 Marmara (sea), Turkey
31/M5 Marquesas (isls.), Fr. Polynesia
12/E3 Marseille, France
30/G3 Marshall Islands
36/F3 Martinique (France)
35/L4 Maryland (state), U.S.
46/E6 Maseru*, Lesotho
21/G1 Mashhad, Iran
35/M3 Massachusetts (state), U.S.
30/H6 Mata Utu*, Wallis & Futuna
34/S9 Maui (isl.), Hawaii
44/C4 Mauritania
7/M7 Mauritius
7/M6 Mayotte, France
46/F6 Mbabane*, Swaziland
7/N8 McDonald (isls.), Australia
34/X12 McKinley (mt.), Alaska
20/C4 Mecca, Saudi Arabia
40/D1 Medellín, Colombia
7/K4 Mediterranean (sea)
23/J5 Mekong (riv.), Asia
30/E5 Melanesia (region), Pacific
29/D4 Melbourne, Australia
36/D2 Mérida, Mexico
20/D2 Mesopotamia (region), Iraq
36/B2 Mexico
36/C3 Mexico (gulf), N. America
36/C3 Mexico City*, Mexico
35/K6 Miami, Florida
35/J3 Michigan (lake), U.S.
35/J2 Michigan (state), U.S.
30/E3 Micronesia (region), Pacific
30/D4 Micronesia, Federated States of
30/H2 Midway Islands (U.S.)
13/F2 Milan, Italy
35/J3 Milwaukee, Wisconsin
31/S12 Mindanao (isl.), Philippines
34/H3 Minneapolis, Minnesota
35/G2 Minnesota (state), U.S.
12/E3 Minorca (Menorca) (isl.), Spain
11/L3 Minsk*, Belarus
35/H5 Mississippi (riv.), U.S.
35/H5 Mississippi (state), U.S.
35/G3 Missouri (riv.), U.S.
35/H4 Missouri (state), U.S.
45/Q7 Mogadishu*, Somalia
11/L5 Moldova
12/E3 Monaco
24/G2 Mongolia
44/C6 Monrovia*, Liberia
34/D2 Montana (state), U.S.
36/B2 Monterrey, Mexico
42/E3 Montevideo*, Uruguay
35/J5 Montgomery*, Alabama
35/K3 Montpelier*, Vermont
37/K5 Montréal, Québec
36/F3 Montserrat (U.K.)
11/J4 Moravia (region), Czech Rep.
44/C1 Morocco
15/E2 Moscow*, Russia
20/D1 Mosul, Iraq
46/G4 Mozambique
10/G4 Munich (München), Germany
29/D4 Murray (riv.), Australia
21/G4 Muscat*, Oman
23/G3 Myanmar

N
25/N5 Nagasaki, Japan
25/Q4 Nagoya, Japan
45/M8 Nairobi*, Kenya
46/C5 Namibia
25/L5 Nanjing (Nanking), China
13/G3 Naples, Italy
35/J4 Nashville*, Tennessee
36/E2 Nassau*, Bahamas
30/F5 Nauru
44/H7 N'Djamena*, Chad
34/F3 Nebraska (state), U.S.
22/D2 Nepal
10/F3 Netherlands
36/F3 Netherlands Antilles
34/C4 Nevada (state), U.S.
37/L5 New Brunswick (prov.), Canada
30/F2 New Caledonia, France
22/D2 New Delhi*, India
37/L4 Newfoundland (prov.), Canada

30/C5 New Guinea (isl.)
35/M3 New Hampshire (state), U.S.
35/M3 New Jersey (state), U.S.
34/E4 New Mexico (state), U.S.
35/H6 New Orleans, Louisiana
35/M3 New York (state), U.S.
35/L3 New York, New York
29/H6 New Zealand
44/G4 Niamey*, Niger
36/D3 Nicaragua
23/F6 Nicobar (isls.), India
20/B1 Nicosia*, Cyprus
44/G4 Niger
44/G6 Niger (riv.), Africa
44/G6 Nigeria
45/M2 Nile (riv.), Africa
31/J7 Niue
15/F2 Nizhniy Novgorod, Russia
30/F7 Norfolk (isl.), Australia
10/E2 North (sea), Europe
33 North America
35/K4 North Carolina (state), U.S.
34/F2 North Dakota (state), U.S.
10/C3 Northern Ireland, U.K.
30/E3 Northern Marianas (U.S.)
25/N3 North Korea
37/N8 Northwest Territories, Canada
14/C3 Norway
38a/F Norwegian (sea), Europe
44/B4 Nouakchott*, Mauritania
30/F7 Nouméa*, New Caledonia
37/L5 Nova Scotia (prov.), Canada
16/J4 Novosibirsk, Russia
31/H7 Nuku'alofa*, Tonga
10/G4 Nürnberg, Germany
37/M3 Nuuk*, Greenland
46/F3 Nyasa (lake), Africa

O
16/G3 Ob' (riv.), Russia
15/D4 Odesa, Ukraine
35/J4 Ohio (riv.), U.S.
35/K3 Ohio (state), U.S.
17/Q4 Okhotsk (sea), Asia
25/N6 Okinawa (isl.), Japan
34/G4 Oklahoma (state), U.S.
35/G4 Oklahoma City*, Oklahoma
34/B2 Olympia*, Washington
21/G4 Oman
21/G4 Oman (gulf), Asia
37/J4 Ontario (prov.), Canada
35/L3 Ontario (lake), N. America
46/C6 Orange (riv.), Africa
34/B2 Oregon (state), U.S.
40/F2 Orinoco (riv.), S. America
25/Q5 Osaka, Japan
14/D4 Oslo*, Norway
37/K5 Ottawa*, Canada
44/E5 Ouagadougou*, Burkina

P
6/B4 Pacific (ocean)
31/H6 Pago Pago*, American Samoa
21/H3 Pakistan
30/C4 Palau
13/G4 Palermo, Italy
36/D4 Panama
36/E4 Panamá*, Panama
31/L6 Papeete*, Fr. Polynesia
30/D5 Papua New Guinea
42/E1 Paraguay
42/E1 Paraguay (riv.), S. America
41/G3 Paramaribo*, Suriname
46/E3 Paraná (riv.), S. America
12/D1 Paris*, France
37/F4 Peace (riv.), Canada
13/H2 Pécs, Hungary
35/L3 Pennsylvania (state), U.S.
15/J2 Perm', Russia
21/G4 Persian (gulf), Asia
29/A4 Perth, Australia
40/C5 Peru
35/L4 Philadelphia, Pennsylvania
31/S10 Philippines
23/H5 Phnom Penh*, Cambodia
31/H5 Phoenix (isls.), Kiribati
34/D5 Phoenix*, Arizona
34/F3 Pierre*, S. Dakota
31/N7 Pitcairn (isl.), U.K.
35/L3 Pittsburgh, Pennsylvania
10/C4 Plymouth, England
13/F2 Po (riv.), Italy
11/J3 Poland
31/J3 Polynesia (region), Pacific
36/E3 Port-au-Prince*, Haiti

7/M7 Port Louis*, Mauritius
30/D5 Port Moresby*, Papua New Guinea
42/F3 Porto Alegre, Brazil
36/F3 Port-of-Spain*, Trinidad & Tobago
44/F5 Porto-Novo*, Benin
12/A4 Portugal
11/H4 Prague (Praha)*, Czech Rep.
46/E6 Pretoria*, S. Africa
37/L5 Prince Edward Isl. (prov.), Canada
35/M3 Providence*, Rhode Island
36/C3 Puebla de Zaragoza, Mexico
36/F3 Puerto Rico (U.S.)
21/K2 Punjab (plain), Asia
25/N5 Pusan, S. Korea
25/N4 P'yŏngyang*, N. Korea
12/C3 Pyrenees (mts.), Europe

Q
20/F3 Qatar
37/K4 Québec (prov.), Canada
37/K5 Québec*, Québec
31/S10 Quezon City, Philippines
40/C4 Quito*, Ecuador

R
44/D1 Rabat*, Morocco
35/L4 Raleigh*, N. Carolina
21/K2 Rawalpindi, Pakistan
41/M5 Recife, Brazil
20/B4 Red (sea)
37/G4 Regina*, Saskatchewan
7/M7 Réunion, France
14/N7 Reykjavík*, Iceland
10/F4 Rhine (riv.), Europe
35/M3 Rhode Island (state), U.S.
12/E2 Rhône (riv.), Europe
35/L4 Richmond*, Virginia
11/L2 Riga*, Latvia
41/K8 Rio de Janeiro, Brazil
34/G6 Rio Grande (riv.), N. America
20/E4 Riyadh*, Saudi Arabia
34/C1 Rocky (mts.), N. America
13/J2 Romania
13/G3 Rome*, Italy
42/D3 Rosario, Argentina
36/F3 Roseau*, Dominica
38b/N Ross (sea), Antarctica
15/E4 Rostov, Russia
10/F4 Rotterdam, Netherlands
20/E5 Rub' al Khali (desert), Asia
16/H3 Russia
46/E1 Rwanda
25/M6 Ryukyu (isls.), Japan

S
34/B4 Sacramento*, California
44/G3 Sahara (desert), Africa
10/C4 St. George's (channel), Europe
36/F3 St. George's*, Grenada
6/J6 St. Helena & Dependencies
36/F3 St. Johns*, Antigua & Barbuda
37/M5 St. John's*, Newfoundland
36/F3 St. Kitts & Nevis
37/L5 St. Lawrence (riv.), N. America
35/H4 St. Louis, Missouri
36/F3 St. Lucia
35/H2 St. Paul*, Minnesota
15/D2 St. Petersburg, Russia
37/M5 St. Pierre & Miquelon (France)
36/F3 St. Vincent & the Grenadines
17/Q4 Sakhalin (isl.), Russia
34/B3 Salem*, Oregon
34/D3 Salt Lake City*, Utah
41/L6 Salvador, Brazil
15/H3 Samara, Russia
20/D5 Sanaa (San'a)*, Yemen
34/C5 San Diego, California
34/B4 San Francisco, California
36/D4 San José*, Costa Rica
36/F3 San Juan*, Puerto Rico
13/G3 San Marino
36/D3 San Salvador*, El Salvador
34/E4 Santa Fe*, New Mexico
42/B3 Santiago*, Chile
36/E3 Santiago de Cuba, Cuba
36/F3 Santo Domingo*, Dominican Rep.
41/J8 São Paulo, Brazil
44/F7 São Tomé and Príncipe
25/R3 Sapporo, Japan
12/C3 Saragossa, Spain
13/H2 Sarajevo*, Bosnia
13/G3 Sardinia (isl.), Italy
37/G4 Saskatchewan (prov.), Canada
20/D4 Saudi Arabia
10/C2 Scotland, U.K.
34/B2 Seattle, Washington
12/D1 Seine (riv.), France

44/B5 Senegal
25/N4 Seoul*, S. Korea
12/B4 Seville, Spain
7/M6 Seychelles
25/M5 Shanghai, China
10/D3 Sheffield, England
25/M3 Shenyang, China
16/K3 Siberia (region), Russia
13/G4 Sicily (isl.), Italy
44/C6 Sierra Leone
45/M2 Sinai (peninsula), Egypt
26/B3 Singapore
13/J3 Skopje*, Macedonia
11/J4 Slovakia
13/G2 Slovenia
31/K6 Society (isls.), Fr. Polynesia
19/E8 Socotra (isl.), Yemen
13/J3 Sofia*, Bulgaria
30/E6 Solomon Islands
45/Q6 Somalia
46/D6 South Africa
40 South America
35/K5 South Carolina (state), U.S.
19/L8 South China (sea), Asia
34/F3 South Dakota (state), U.S.
42/J7 South Georgia (isl.), U.K.
25/N4 South Korea
38b/W South Orkney (isls.), U.K.
12/B3 Spain
35/J4 Springfield*, Illinois
22/D6 Sri Lanka
42/E7 Stanley*, Falkland Isls.
14/F4 Stockholm*, Sweden
12/E1 Strasbourg, France
10/G4 Stuttgart, Germany
40/E7 Sucre*, Bolivia
45/L5 Sudan
45/M1 Suez (canal), Egypt
31/R11 Sulu (sea), Asia
26/B4 Sumatra (isl.), Indonesia
35/J2 Superior (lake), N. America
26/D5 Surabaya, Indonesia
41/G3 Suriname
30/G6 Suva*, Fiji
16/B2 Svalbard (isls.), Norway
46/F6 Swaziland
14/E3 Sweden
12/E2 Switzerland
29/E4 Sydney, Australia
20/C1 Syria
11/H3 Szczecin, Poland

T
15/G6 Tabriz, Iran
12/B4 Tagus (riv.), Europe
31/L6 Tahiti (isl.), Fr. Polynesia
25/M6 Taipei*, Taiwan
25/M7 Taiwan (Rep. of China)
16/H6 Tajikistan
24/C4 Takla Makan (desert), China
35/K5 Tallahassee*, Florida
14/H4 Tallinn*, Estonia
46/F2 Tanganyika (lake), Africa
44/D1 Tangier, Morocco
46/F2 Tanzania
30/G4 Tarawa*, Kiribati
16/G5 Tashkent*, Uzbekistan
30/E8 Tasman (sea), Pacific
29/D5 Tasmania (isl.), Australia
15/D6 Taurus (mts.), Turkey
15/F5 Tbilisi*, Georgia
20/F1 Tehran*, Iran
20/B2 Tel Aviv-Yafo, Israel
35/J4 Tennessee (state), U.S.
36/D3 Tegucigalpa*, Honduras
34/G5 Texas (state), U.S.
23/H4 Thailand
23/H5 Thailand (gulf), Asia
13/J3 Thessaloníki, Greece
22/E2 Thimphu*, Bhutan
25/L5 Tianjin (Tientsin), China
24/C3 Tian Shan (mts.), Asia
24/D5 Tibet (region), China
20/E2 Tigris (riv.), Asia
36/A1 Tijuana, Mexico
27/F5 Timor (isl.), Indonesia
13/H3 Tiranë*, Albania
40/E7 Titicaca (lake), S. America
44/F6 Togo
31/H5 Tokelau, New Zealand
25/Q4 Tokyo*, Japan
31/H7 Tonga
23/J4 Tonkin (gulf), Asia
35/G4 Topeka*, Kansas
37/K5 Toronto*, Ontario
36/B2 Torreón, Mexico
30/D6 Torres (strait)
12/D2 Tours, France
35/M3 Trenton*, New Jersey
13/G2 Trieste, Italy
40/F1 Trinidad and Tobago
44/H1 Tripoli*, Libya
6/J7 Tristan da Cunha (isl.), St. Helena
22/C6 Trivandrum, India
30/E4 Truk (isls.), Micronesia

44/H1 Tunis*, Tunisia
44/G1 Tunisia
12/E2 Turin, Italy
15/D6 Turkey
16/F6 Turkmenistan
36/E2 Turks & Caicos Isls. (U.K.)
30/G5 Tuvalu
13/F4 Tyrrhenian (sea), Europe

U
16/F4 Ufa, Russia
45/M7 Uganda
15/C4 Ukraine
24/J2 Ulaanbaatar*, Mongolia
20/F4 United Arab Emirates
10/C3 United Kingdom
34 United States
16/F5 Ural (riv.), Asia
16/F3 Ural (mts.), Russia
42/E3 Uruguay
34/D4 Utah (state), U.S.
24/E3 Ürümqi (Urumchi), China
34/D4 Utah (state), U.S.
16/G5 Uzbekistan

V
13/F2 Vaduz*, Liechtenstein
13/C4 Valencia, Spain
42/B3 Valparaíso, Chile
37/E5 Vancouver, Br. Columbia
30/F6 Vanuatu
13/G3 Vatican City
40/E2 Venezuela
13/G2 Venice (Venezia), Italy
36/C3 Veracruz, Mexico
35/M3 Vermont (state), U.S.
45/M8 Victoria (lake), Africa
37/E5 Victoria*, Br. Columbia
37/F2 Victoria (isl.), N.W. Territories
13/H1 Vienna*, Austria
23/H4 Vientiane*, Laos
23/J5 Vietnam
30/F6 Vila*, Vanuatu
11/L3 Vilnius*, Lithuania
35/L4 Virginia (state), U.S.
36/F3 Virgin Isls. (U.K., U.S.)
25/P3 Vladivostok, Russia
15/G4 Volga (riv.), Russia
15/F4 Volgograd, Russia
40/E6 Volta (lake), Ghana

W
30/F3 Wake (isl.), U.K.
10/C3 Wales, U.K.
30/G6 Wallis & Futuna (France)
11/K3 Warsaw*, Poland
34/B2 Washington (state), U.S.
35/L4 Washington, D.C.*, U.S.
29/H7 Wellington*, New Zealand
20/C2 West Bank
44/B3 Western Sahara
31/H6 Western Samoa
36/D3 West Indies
35/K4 West Virginia (state), U.S.
16/D3 White (sea), Russia
37/D3 Whitehorse*, Yukon
34/C4 Whitney (mt.), California
40/E1 Willemstad*, Neth. Antilles
46/C5 Windhoek*, Namibia
37/H5 Winnipeg (cap.), Manitoba
35/H3 Wisconsin (state), U.S.
11/J4 Wrocław, Poland
25/K5 Wuhan, China
34/E3 Wyoming (state), U.S.

X
24/D3 Xinjiang (region), China
41/H4 Xingu (riv.), Brazil

Y
17/N3 Yakutsk, Russia
25/M3 Yalu (riv.), China
44/D6 Yamoussoukro*, Côte d'Ivoire
21/G4 Yangon* (Rangoon), Myanmar
44/H7 Yaoundé*, Cameroon
16/G4 Yekaterinburg, Russia
25/M4 Yellow (sea), Asia
37/F3 Yellowknife*, N.W. Territories
20/E5 Yemen
16/J3 Yenisey (riv.), Russia
15/F5 Yerevan*, Armenia
25/Q4 Yokohama, Japan
36/D3 Yucatán (peninsula), Mexico
13/J3 Yugoslavia
37/F3 Yukon (territory), Canada
33/B3 Yukon (riv.), N. America

Z
13/H2 Zagreb*, Croatia
20/E1 Zagros (mts.), Iran
46/C2 Zaire
46/F4 Zambezi (riv.), Africa
46/E3 Zambia
46/G2 Zanzibar (isl.), Tanzania
46/E4 Zimbabwe
12/F2 Zürich, Switzerland